JFDP -

Reflections of Eurasian Scholars

Edited by Zeeshan-ul-hassan Usmani
with
Tatyana Shadieva and Imran Khanzada

Bloomington, IN  Milton Keynes, UK

authorHOUSE®

AuthorHouse™
1663 Liberty Drive, Suite 200
Bloomington, IN 47403
www.authorhouse.com
Phone: 1-800-839-8640

AuthorHouse™ UK Ltd.
500 Avebury Boulevard
Central Milton Keynes, MK9 2BE
www.authorhouse.co.uk
Phone: 08001974150

First published by AuthorHouse 1/23/2007

ISBN: 978-1-4259-7423-7 (sc)

Printed in the United States of America
Bloomington, Indiana

This book is printed on acid-free paper.

"Research for the essays included in this book was supported in part by the Junior Faculty Development Program, a program of the Bureau of Educational and Cultural Affairs (ECA) of the United States Department of State, under authority of the Fulbright-Hays Act of 1961 as amended and administered by American Councils for International Education: ACTR/ACCELS. The content and accuracy of the works included in this publication are solely the responsibilities of the authors, and the opinions expressed herein are the authors' own and do not necessarily express the views of either ECA or American Councils."

Izzat Khanu – My Mother Who Taught Me When to Say No
~Zeeshan-ul-hassan Usmani

To My Mom, Who Always Believes in Me and Supports Me in All
My Endeavors
~Tatyana Shadieva

To My Family, and Especially My Mother, Who Gave Me Precious
Memories
~Imran Khanzada

Preface

"Embracing diversity is one adventure after another, opening new paths of discovery that connect an understanding to caring, listening, and sharing with others who are different than ourselves."

~ April Holland

Today, not many of us remember the Cold War and the separation of globe into two blocks: the Socialist camp and the Capitalist camp. After Perestroika in the late 1980s and the collapse of Soviet Union in the early 1990s, the window of opportunity to Europe and the US was opened once again for the people of the former block. World changed altogether and the Eurasian youth were given a chance to participate in various exchange programs, travel abroad and gain new experiences.

Although many of us today take these experiences for granted, there are others, such as Eurasian scholars who have to struggle to get such opportunities. Therefore, while for some, it is just a different experience in their lives, for others, it is a life changing experience for being abroad for the first time.

The Junior Faculty Development Program (JFDP) is an exchange program tailored for early career scholars and professionals. JFDP program allows young scholars to experience and learn from American classrooms. The participants see teaching as a process of observing, active listening, and learn various subjects from diverse perspectives. The JFDP scholarships also offer young scholars to participate in professional events like conferences, forums and discussions. By living in the United States these scholars gain a first hand experience of American life, its culture, people and society.

Every year, the American Council/ACCELS organizes an educational fair to introduce different programs sponsored by US Department of States. Since majority of the JFDP alumni are not able to participate in this fair, we felt the need of a book that includes personal essays by JFDP alumni from Eurasian countries to share their wonderful experiences with coming JFDP scholars. This anthology shares the interesting, surprising, and sometime naïve stories of JFDP alumni. This work is first of its kind in JFDP family of scholars.

While selecting essays for this collection, we thought about what might most interest our readers. The most important criterion we decided was the wider representation of different aspects of academic and cultural life in the

USA. We leave it to our readers to draw their conclusions and judge the tales of scholars. Our goal is to simply share the experiences of JFDP alumni and give new scholars a unique chance to look at the USA from the eyes of their fellow citizens, who gained extraordinary experiences that not only changed them forever, but also brought new ideas to their home universities.

Editors would like to thank the contributors for their fondness to share their stories and their enthusiasm to encourage aspiring JFDP fellows. And, our gratitude to Junior Faculty Development Program (JFDP) program alumni and offices in respective countries for their guidance and support extended to this book project.

Editors

Contents

An Affair to Remember

Larissa Chuprina, PhD

– Ukraine –

My "affair" with the Junior Faculty Development Program began unexpectedly. I learned about this opportunity for professional development through a local office in Kharkiv, Ukraine, just four days before the deadline to apply as a candidate. I was really lucky with cooperative colleagues and former professors of mine who promptly wrote letters of recommendations for me and provided a computer, still a rare thing in offices at that time. I did not have a personal computer and I had no computer skills. Nevertheless, I managed to write down all the necessary information and the Statement of Intent — an essay-plan for the hypothetical program in the USA--as a requirement to participate in the competition. Though I thought my chances were slim, I still decided to try this opportunity for a chance to pursue professional development in the USA. This was something I had been dreaming about since my graduation from Kharkiv State University, Foreign Languages Department.

At the time of application for the Junior Faculty Development Program, I was the Director and owner of a Language School with Educational Tourism that enabled language immersion for our students. The Junior Faculty Development Program would be a great opportunity for my immersion in an English-speaking country and for the development of other skills needed in International Education and Educational Administration.

A couple of months later, the selection committee informed me that I was among the finalists. It took some time for them to make a decision about the placement, as I was interested in Educational and Business Administration, and not just Language Education. Finally, I was placed at The University of Tennessee in Knoxville, TN. Together with several other scholars; I was on my way to the point of destination in August 1996. Arriving there on my birthday, I began a new phase of my life in the south of the U.S.A. together with professional affiliation with the Department of Management, College of Business and Administration of the University of Tennessee.

We were welcomed by the Director of the Central and Eastern Europe Center, who took responsibility for seven JFDP scholars. He was also the founder and the President of the Alliance of Universities for Democracy that had started its honorable work years before the break-out of the Soviet Union, with the hope to bring democracy to Eastern Europe through higher education and through collaboration between educators of the USA and Central and Eastern Europe. It looked like our office was the center of the world, as all the roads led to our Center, where our scholars became a local attraction and made a splash in a quiet town.

Cultural Adjustment

The seven scholars, all females from Russia and Ukraine, in the Center were very compatible and friendly with each other, sharing one room and four computers in the office. We shared our knowledge and skills, too. Three of us were good with English, and other girls were good with computers. Everybody was good at something that was brought to a common use in our intellectual Pot Luck. We traded our expertise and helped each other in acquiring new necessary skills. We provided psychological support to each other, too, by sharing ideas and spending time together. That was important during the period of cultural adjustment. We also made many American friends, hosting them in our homes or being their guests on different occasions.

With the help of another person who was on the staff in the Center, the Program Manager, and who was our main cultural informant, none of us had a severe case of culture shock. We had a good time, studying, observing the culture, participating in different activities, but also getting in trouble together.

"Trouble" was what happened during our first month in the USA. We were having a house-warming party at my place, as I got an apartment close to the campus, while the rest of the scholars were on a waiting list. Of course, all the scholars from the Center were invited. It was not until midnight that we realized that we did not know how the guests could get back to their apartments, which were quite a distance from my new place. In the daytime, there was a bus service, and we were not aware of the limitations of the public transportation in Knoxville.

The bus that brought them to my place had stopped running at 8 p.m., and no other public transportation was available after 10 p.m. No one had a car or a driving license. We needed to find a way out of the situation. Then, two of the girls recalled a piece of information that sounded like a revelation and a good way out. Somebody told them that calling 911 could bring a van service to the door of the student housing. One of the bravest girls decided to be a contact person, dialing these magic digits. To her and our surprise the voice answered: "Police." Our friend hung up, not knowing what to say. We needed a van service! We made several attempts to dial the same number that seemed to be our salvation, instead, we heard the same greeting "Police." Thinking that this was not what we needed, we decided to get out of the apartment to look for somebody who might have a car and could give the guests a ride to their place.

But as soon as we came out of the apartment, we saw about 10 policemen crawling along the wall, armed with guns, with intent to break into my apartment, which we had just left, in response to multiple calls to the police. They thought that somebody was kidnapped and could not talk! However, the police, seeing our festive mood and our friendly disposition, combined with our genuine surprise at the scene, put down the guns to negotiate with us peacefully. After listening to our explanation, the police officers, as friendly as they could be, offered our girls a ride. Several fine looking girls climbed in. It was a solution, except their car had a very low entrance with bars (to make it difficult for suspects to escape). Well, it was not a limo, but it was a service we needed and appreciated. The officers had a chuckle, escorting "Slavic beauties" to the police car. For a quiet southern town we were exotic and brought a high degree of novelty.

The next morning, the first thing we saw in the lobby of the housing were flyers with information about van service, its hours, and telephone numbers (that were not there before and were different from the number we were dialing). And… the local newspaper published a small note in a crime log section about the incident (Thank goodness, not accident! No names were mentioned, either). I still have a clip of this note somewhere in my papers, as a souvenir from those days and our first encounter with the U.S. police, which turned out to be very friendly and helpful under circumstances.

Beyond Academic Life

We had other interesting encounters with people from different walks of life, position, social status, age, and gender in the academic setting and beyond. Everyone expressed a genuine interest in us as people from the "evil" empire. However, our similarities were more evident than cultural differences, when looked at a deeper level. We found commonalities, when conversing about our families or feelings, concerns about economy, politics, ecology, education, and other matters that constituted our life. We experienced such a warm reception in their homes and hearts that it was difficult to think how we could live without each other all those years and that soon we would separate. I am still in touch with most of them, ten years later, thanks to technology.

We learned that Americans were hard-working people, sincere and sometimes naïve, some more religious than others, and ready to show their volunteer spirit. It was so different from the America presented in the movies or through mass media. We witnessed a different America, through people we worked with or socialized at different events, or through members of their families who also became our friends.

Celebrations of Thanksgiving, Christmas, and Easter with our American colleagues and friends enlarged our knowledge about the history and culture of our host country. Traditional meals with family and friends helped us find a common ground we all share: humanity, dreams, joys and fears to bond people together in friendship and understanding, inspirations and hardships. We all share this planet Earth–our home–and, if something happens to it, we all will face the consequences.

The knowledge, skills and attitudes that I learned during my Fellowship have been serving me since and helping me now when I teach Intercultural Communication at a university level or through professional training for business people. I learned that respect to other cultures and learning from them, without forgetting our roots and cultural background, can enrich our lives and bring personal and spiritual growth.

Where is Ukraine?

This was a frequent question at that time. In 1996-1997, Ukraine was not well known globally or historically as a culture or a country. Ukraine reclaimed it sovereignty in August 1991. The country has a long cultural tradition, dating 7,000 years back, but a short history of statehood in modern times. During the Program, we had an opportunity as scholars to share information about our native country. Another scholar from Lviv, a city located in the West of Ukraine, and I, from Kharkiv in the East, became a team to promote knowledge about our country in Knoxville and beyond. The University of

Tennessee Library generously gave us permission to use one of their display cases for some Ukrainian cultural artifacts, such as embroidered table runner, Pysanky (Ukrainian decorated Easter eggs) and facts about Ukraine under the title "DO YOU KNOW THAT...?". This exposition lasted for a month, bringing more people to our circle, many of whom became our friends. First of all, we were discovering Ukraine to ourselves, reading accounts about glorious and tragic pages in its history as told by historians. We were eager to share its story with others.

On one occasion, we gave a big presentation about Ukraine in the International House attended by more than 100 guests. We were proud of our country that had just celebrated its 4th anniversary of independence. Preparing for the presentation, we found many books on history of Ukraine that were not available in the former Soviet Union or independent Ukraine. We had discovered Ukraine ourselves.

Another effort to bring awareness about Ukraine was to teach its language and culture. The same Ukrainian friend-colleague in the Program and I were auditing the course "Methods in Teaching Foreign Languages" which prompted us to develop and teach four lessons on the Ukrainian Language and Culture for middle school students. Ukrainian rhymes, songs, story telling, role playing, music, dances, art, and real Ukrainian food-- varenyky (dumplings) and compot (fruit drink) were part of our syllabus. We created a list of common Ukrainian phrases and provided historical and cultural information as hand-outs. We used the Ukrainian flag colors—blue (for the sky) and yellow (for wheat, rye, and sunflowers) for visual aids and decorations. These lessons became unexpectedly popular, and soon invitations came from different schools as well. We even traveled outside Tennessee on this mission.

Other Learning Opportunities

The three scholars from our Center, including the author, were invited as honorary members of Knoxville Marketing Association which met monthly on the 26th floor of the tallest building in Knoxville. The meetings included a luncheon with guest speakers coupled with socialization and networking for business people. It was difficult for me to listen and eat simultaneously. In Ukraine, it is considered rude to chew when someone is speaking.

As we realized, in the business world, time is money, so people eat during presentations, allowing participants to be back to work shortly after the lunch time. For a couple of months, I left hungry, unable to finish eating before the end of the event. Besides listening to speakers, we were also invited to share our world view and expected to talk, while eating. I was trying hard to become more multifunctional in this area of communication. I also had to keep my thoughts and emotions to myself during conversation, waiting for my turn to speak, and learned not to overlap with the person I was talking to, something that is common in the Eastern European culture.

An Important Cultural Event

The biggest social event at The University of Tennessee and in Knoxville in general was the football game. This, we had to experience and see the university team *Vols* (stands for Volunteers) in action. This event usually brings generations together for tailgating before the game and after, either to celebrate or to mourn. The games are played in the fall, when even trees wear costumes of yellow and orange, the colors of the local team. On one of sunny and warm days of the fall, real Indian summer, the department gave us tickets to a football game, so that we could witness the socio-cultural event that should not be missed even by foreigners.

My Ukrainian friend and I went together to see this game of American football. We expected that it would be different from soccer, which is very popular among Ukrainians. After enjoying a picturesque parade on the streets before the game, we arrived at the stadium, the largest athletic complex in the state for non-professional football; we found our seats and were ready to watch the game. Half an hour later, not understanding the game's rules or where the ball was supposed to go for points, I peacefully fell asleep. And though the fans were far from quiet, reacting boisterously to any successful or faulty pass or kick, the warm sun and a busy schedule of a JFDP scholar made the noisy stadium an ideal place to relax and recreate. I never confessed this faux pas to any die hard Vols fans for the fear of offending those who claimed that even their blood was orange!

Besides resting well, I was really impressed with the order and amiable disposition of American fans during and after the game. Though the players behaved tough on the field, the people around did not show any aggression or agitation towards the fans of the rival team. We observed that many couples were wearing the colors of the opposing teams, yet were holding hands and smiling at each other. After the game, the crowd just quickly dissolved, without causing any traffic jam or inconveniences. Though the stadium and the streets were covered with trash from food and drinks, the morning after the game everything was nicely cleaned.

We learned that football for many Americans is an inspiration and life celebration. The field is the place where people can display their best values: optimism, solidarity, teamwork, leadership, and perseverance in achieving a goal.

Being a JFDP Alumna

My Fellowship also enabled me to attend many enlightening conferences in different parts of the United States. Soon I learned how to use a computer and how to drive a car. I became more proficient in the American English Language (We were educated in British English in school in secondary and higher education), which opened the way to useful and important things about American culture and history.

Formal or informal encounters with professionals and lay people did impact my professional and personal development and contributed to my understanding of the meaning of the program. These people helped me grasp a sense of life and of myself.

My trip to America was a journey to myself. Somewhere I read that we know ourselves better through encounters with other people, especially different from us. How true!

During the farewell party at the end of the program, the Director of the Hodges Library of The University of Tennessee and also the advisor of several of our scholars noted that the hosting university had learned from us more than they had given. It was very rewarding to know that we were leaving our legacy with the University of Tennessee and that we had contributed to the decision to keep the program running. Several of us went to Washington, DC to talk to Congressmen and to convince them in the importance of the program for the American side and for visiting scholars. The Director pointed to the real value of this exchange program which was learning from each other. The Program provided the framework for exchanging knowledge, skills, ideas, and goodwill between people and countries.

The Junior Faculty Development Program (JFDP) has definitely developed my professional skills as an educator. What is more, it has made me more aware of how our lives are intertwined in this world. This program has made me truly a citizen of the world. Now, ten years after this wonderful experience of being a scholar, I see my duty in building bridges between cultures through languages and openness about different cultures, regardless of what I teach and where I teach. My experience with the JFDP remains an "affair" to remember.

Personal Reflections on the Effects of the Junior Faculty Development Program

Pavel V. Sysoyev, PhD, Ed.D.

– Russia –

$\mathcal{G}$am from a city called Tambov, located about 300 miles to the south-east from Moscow. Its population is about half a million citizens, which makes it an average size city according to the Russian standards. Tambov State University named after G.R. Derzhavin is the biggest university in the whole region and is the place of my employment. I am currently a professor of American & British Studies and Applied Linguistics at the Faculty of Modern Languages and director of the Foreign Language Poly-cultural Education Research Laboratory. As English and American Studies are my major areas of expertise, I was fortunate to study and do my doctoral research in the United States on a few occasions: in 1994-1995 at the University of South Alabama as an American Councils for International Education (ACTR/ACCELS) undergraduate exchange student, in 1998 at the University of Indiana, and in 1998-1999 at the Pennsylvania State University as a President Boris Yeltsin's research scholar. In 2001-2002 I was invited to spend an academic year at the University of Iowa (Iowa City) as a JFDP fellow and a visiting research professor. Even though the year I was on JFDP was not my first visit to the US, the experience I had was really exceptional and is worth sharing with my colleagues from the rest of the world.

Academic Collaboration with the US Colleagues and Students

As a part of the JFDP, scholars are to audit several classes at their host institutions, i.e. attend and sit together with the US students, do all assignments, and participate in class discussions. That was exactly what I did at the University of Iowa, which hosted me for 2001-2002 academic years. I took several social science courses connected with American Studies and Personal Identity. All of them included extensive discussions of various social and cultural issues such as racism, classism, ableism, homophobia, sexism, stereotypes and the media. Coming from a different country and having a different educational and cultural experience, comparing to the rest of the students, inevitably I often had different views and opinions on the issues addressed in classes. Participating in group discussions with the US students I was always glad to share my views and explain where my opinions come from. The US students, in return, were able to hear another voice and be able to see that different cultural background have effects on the world views of people. Through the discussion we all were able to see similarities and differences in our opinions. That dialogue was very efficient and beneficial for our growth, maturity, and development of the world view. Seeing the nature of these differences in different backgrounds through group discussions we all (Russian JFDP fellows, American and foreign students in classes) were able to take *diversity as a norm* of cultural coexistence in the modern multicultural Russian, American, and other societies.

Similar mutual sharing and learning took place during our professional collaboration with the US mentors and colleagues. Introduction of the Russian scholarship and learning about research of my American colleagues enabled to identify state-of-the-art of the target research issues, which is essential in the development of unified research. Very productive and mutually interesting in this respect are joint research projects. I was fortunate to co-conduct research with a professor from Penn State Dr Sandra J. Savignon, who served as my academic advisor, when I conducted my MA and PhD. research. It turned out that we have similar professional interests, but use different theories and scholarships to support the arguments. Our experience proved to be fruitful and positive. The results of our studies have been published in such US professional refereed journals as *The Modern Language Journal* and *Foreign Language Annals*. From my experience I would say that joint research projects which combine and intertwine Russian and US scholarship are of great interest to the US professional audience, who is unfamiliar with works by the Russian scholars published in Russian. Joint research enables Russian scholars to find and show the niche they take in the world science in their field.

American Cultural Studies Curriculum and Teaching Materials Development

Being in the US on JFDP, I developed an American Cultural Studies Curriculum (university level) and wrote a textbook "Multicultural America: Teaching about Cultural Diversity of the United States" (Moscow, Euro-school Press, 2005). All cultural themes and topics are presented in the curriculum and in the textbook through the "cultural diversity" framework, i.e. each issue is addressed from various perspectives and from the angles of different social groups. For example, when studying about social class in the United States, students are given information not only about the life of white, Anglo-Saxon, middle class, employed, able Americans, but also learn about the lifestyle and opportunities for the future of the representatives of other social groups based on race/ethnicity, social class, gender, physical ability, age, and other such biographical information. This way learner gets a better understanding of the modern multicultural US society.

The uniqueness of the textbook is also in its content. It is the first textbook published in Russia, which addresses such issues as race, ethnicity and racism, social class and classism, cultural privileges and cultural oppression, stereotypes and the media, sexual orientation and homophobia, gender and sexism, disabilities and ableism, interrelation between language and culture. When I piloted this textbook with my students at the Tambov State University, I was blessed to get very positive responses. Here is what one of my students wrote in his reflective journal at the end of the American Cultural Studies course:

> "... I began to think about things, which used to be invisible to me– different kinds of diversity in every society (ethnic, religious, political, social), prejudices about some minority groups, and privileges of other groups, oppression and discrimination. I never thought about it before as a representative of the majority. This class made me look differently on what is happening around me. ..." (Unpublished data from P.V. Sysoyev, 2003; for further details about the experiment, see Sysoyev, 2003).

Discussing modern US society, students were able to make analogies to the Russian society. This reflection made them see their own country and city as a multicultural place where people of different cultural groups (based on ethnicity, social class, ability, gender, etc.) get involved into intercultural contact on a daily basis. The ability to see the difference is the first step to the development of tolerance and empathy towards diversity. And I am glad that my course and materials I developed being on JFDP served as a spring board for my students in their life-long journey of the development of their identity and tolerance to diversity.

Many of the ideas and materials developed in the US were also applied in the American Cultural Studies Curriculum for secondary schools (10-11 grades, profile level) (co-authored with V. Safonova) and two parts of the textbook "US Culture and Society" (co-authored with V. Safonova). This curriculum and textbook got recommendation of the Russian Ministry of Education and Science to be used as federal textbooks of American Studies in secondary schools (see references at the end of the paper).

Terrorist Attack of 9/11

Terrorist attack of 9/11 took place about two weeks after we arrived. At that time I did not have a TV set, so I first learned about it when I came to one of my morning classes. I took my seat and I heard students were describing what was happening. At first I did not pay much attention, as I though they were discussing the latest blockbuster. But their emotional discourse caught my attention and made me ask for the name of the movie. Unfortunately that was not fiction, but terrifying reality.

The class started with the discussion of the latest news. The professor made everyone speak out and express his/her thoughts. Discussing terrorism, one of the students asked me to reflect on the situation in Chechnya. I did share with the rest of the class and later with many people I interacted in the US what the Russian government had to go through with terrorist groups in Chechnya and in different other place in my country. Through that discussion we all got to the idea that terrorism is a global problem. Not a single country can resolve it solely without support of the world community. Therefore, all nations should unite, understand, collaborate, and support each other to win a victory over world terrorism.

Now, looking backwards and reflecting on what was really happen on our subconscious level, I think we all needed support and understanding of "others"–"outsiders" and "foreigners". It was important for me–a foreigner from Russia–to get support and understanding from the common Americans, who have just experienced acts of terrorism. It was also important for them– "insiders"–to get support from me as a representative of the country, which had been dealing with terrorism for a long time. We gave each other support and that was helpful.

Slavic Bazaar

In April 2002, Office of the International Programs in conjunction with the Center for Russian, East European, and Eurasian Studies at the University of Iowa, which hosted JFDP fellows, organized a cultural event to celebrate Slavic countries and cultures. All guests were able to enjoy traditional Russian and Slavic food, music, puppet show, staged by the community of immigrants from the former USSR. JFDP fellows made posters about their home countries (Russia, Ukraine, and Belarus) and gave presentations about them to teenagers from the local junior high schools.

That event was very important to us, because it was a good chance to show that we are different and we are here. Lecturing to Americans and representing our Slavic countries and cultures we felt as cultural bridges between our nations. What politicians cannot sometimes do, common people can do well.

Identity, Culture, and Language Teaching

In 2001-2002, being a JFDP fellow I initiated a publishing project and served as an editor of the volume of research papers entitles "Identity, Culture, and Language Teaching." Twenty four JFDP scholars responded to my invitation and contributed papers dealing with various aspects of the "language, culture, and identity" tracheotomy. The book was published with the University of Iowa Center for Russian, East European and Eurasian Studies and it is the only book in the field of Applied Linguistics/TESOL, which presents to the English speaking scholars the research of Russian scholars. The purpose was similar to other events we took part in—share with the US colleagues the findings of our research studies.

JFDP Alumni Events

I am glad that after the completion of the program in the US, American Councils for International Education ACTR/ACCELS on the regular basis continue to keep in touch with JFDP alumni, arranging various JFDP alumni events. I personally participated in two kinds of such events: *Local Initiative Grant Program* and *University Round Tables.*

With the help of the Local Initiative Grant Program in Fall 2003, at the Tambov State University I organized and conducted an international conference "Teaching Foreign Languages in the Global Cross-Cultural Space". The event aimed to address current issues in co-teaching a foreign language with a foreign culture. About 10 JFDP alumni made presentations for 200 participants from various Russian and foreign universities. At the end a volume of papers was published and distributed to the departments of foreign languages throughout Russia.

Another event, which is worth mentioning in this paper, is University Round Tables. It is a two hour meetings devoted to current educational issues. Meetings take place once or twice a month. As guest speakers JFDP office invited leading experts in the field of education and policy making. Each presentation ended up with a Question and Answer session. Thus, all participants of the University Round Tables were able to get first-hand knowledge on the current issues and inform our local faculty about that. I participated in a several of such meetings devoted to the discussion of the

Unified Exam, introduction of the two-stage educational system (bachelor's and master's degrees versus five-year diplomas) based on the Bologna agreement.

As I mentioned before, the advantage of the JFDP alumni events as well as JFDP itself is that it functions with a *multiplier* effect. Selected for each meeting individuals get together, learn about certain educational issues, get back to their home institutions and immediately spread the news locally.

Conclusion

Junior Faculty Development Program is a very special and unique program for the university faculty from Russia and a few other East European countries. As I tried to show in this paper, it is beneficial to all parties involved. In addition, JFDP fellows have a privilege to interact with a very kind, responsive, and understanding ACTR/ACCELS specialists in Washington, D.C., who with their advice and wisdom help you feel at home during your stay in the United States. I wish JFDP good luck and prosperity. And to those university teachers who are considering applying for an exchange program, JFDP is the right choice.

Through a Superficial Diversity to an Intrinsic Harmony

Azim Bayzoev, PhD

– Tajikistan –

$\mathcal{J}$arrived in Kansas together with the other participants of the Junior Faculty Development Program (American Councils' Program for International Education–ACTR-ACCELS) at the beginning of December. This was a program for special training to improve one's English knowledge. After the month-long courses in KU and a three-day orientation conference in Washington DC, I returned to my host university, the University of Kansas, to carry out my research. First of all, I would like to express my gratitude to the JFDP Office Staff in Washington, its branch in Tajikistan, our remarkable professors from EAC, the faculty of the International Program, my academic adviser, the faculty of the Women's Studies Program, the library staff, and all those with whom I worked, talked, and shared opinions. I am grateful for the friendly welcome, help and cooperation. I really liked Lawrence and KU. The majority of my colleagues, who have left KU after English courses, are also of the opinion that Lawrence is one of the best places.

However, I am not going to talk about my project and research at KU now; rather, I want to talk about differences and similarities among peoples based on my observations since coming to America.

In Dushanbe, Tajikistan, where I am from, during the pre-orientation meeting we were informed that America, American culture, and the American people are completely different from Tajiks, and we should pay close attention to these distinctions. We arrived in Lawrence, and again we were told about distinctions - in traditions, life style, behavior, language, history, etc. When we were at the Orientation Conference in Washington in early January, many presentations were also devoted to distinctions between groups and categories of people, the educational systems of the different countries, etc.

Coming back to Lawrence, I, as well as others, chose classes to attend. And there, again, basically, it was a question of distinctions - about the features of styles of speech, reading, and writing of women writers, how gender problems appear in various parts of the world. Even on the term "violence," just one word, we put different interpretations depending on the region of the world we are discussing. I read a remarkable book by Deborah Tannen, *You Just Don't Understand* —here too it is about various distinctions between women and men in conversation. When we are talking with people from the different countries, again a key question is: "What about yours?"—Certainly, a hint on how you are different. Even harmless, simple daily questions used in practically any educational context all over the world—"Any other comments? Or "Have you anything else to add?"—invite differences in opinion. One gains the impression that there are a lot of distinctions in our lives, rather than similarities. It seems that the distinctions between us are so important that we only want to study differences.

Nevertheless, being in a different culture and society, observing people, attending classes, wandering through streets and shops, watching TV, reading books and newspapers, tasting different meals from different nations, I have not experienced any culture shock! Rather, I have met people who share more similarities with me than differences. The reason was that I didn't intentionally focus on differences, I always thought about our similarities! Let's think: we like to say that our educational systems are different from each other. But at the same time, it is certain that the more than 1500 foreign students studying at KU do not differ in any great respect from their American contemporaries— either in study or in public life. But they have received secondary education in their home countries, as you like to say, under various conditions. Do you hint at any distinctions? But a lot of differences can be found even among American students too, if they are considered separately. Do you find the close relation in interpreting between "diversity" and "separateness"?

I have found much in common between our (Tajik) and American students–that they equally aspire to be successful and knowledgeable and to graduate. I am assured, if the language barrier can be excluded (for example, take my son, a student whose English is very good); they will find a common language very quickly when meeting Americans of the same age, despite the many differences that have been ascribed to them.

We have gotten used to saying that we speak in different languages, forgetting that very often no two people speaking the same language can *understand* each other, and there can be many close friends speaking different languages. We teach our students math, for instance, with very different languages, but the result of teaching (the students' acquiring knowledge and experience) usually is the same. We speak in amazement of the many varieties of bread in the world (you can imagine how many different meals there could be in the world!); often forgetting that everywhere they are made of the same materials. And the word "tasty" as a measure of quality is identical, accepted by all without exception. We can analyze the sacred books of various religions and find that probably more than 70% (and likely much more) of their contents would be equal.

Distinctions, certainly, exist, and they are really valid. But in general all of them are about form, not content. If so, is it necessary for us to focus attention only on presence of distinctions that at will we could easily interpret as disagreements? In other words, is the form really more important than the content?

Why Would I Like to Tell About This Now?

This is my second time in America. The first time I was to come here in October, 2001, but in the aftermath of September 11th I had to postpone my visit until spring 2002 (As we can see, these events concerned me too, though I didn't have any connection with them. And there are many people like me). At that time, flying by plane for more than 10 hours without landing, I involuntary began to think about those events and composed a verse on this theme (it has been published in our newspaper, and also in a collection of my verse). The gist of this verse is as follows:

When I flew high and saw all the beauty of our planet, I started to admire the intellect and skill of mankind. Human reason had become a creator, and creating miracles has transformed our world into paradise. But when the plane came nearer to America I saw in front of me another world - the world of destructions and wars. I found out the double force of human reason - creative and destructive. Manhattan has been both constructed and destroyed by human reason. How can I be proud of human reason and its force in general after that? I will be proud of human reason only when I see Jews and Moslems living together in peace again; when I see all continents like brothers or like children of one Mother, the Earth; when I see a world without wars, without parents' tears, and all nations of the world as believers of the unique God, the Founder of the Universe. If mankind really possesses such a powerful force as reason, it should construct a universal, common and free "World House" for all people built of bricks made by love of humanity.

Certainly, in my native Tajik language, where I have observed all the rules of versification, it sounds different and better. But as I already mentioned, the content is more important than the form.

Being in America for the second time, I have started again to think of those events. The reasons might be different. One might be because this year exactly five years will have passed. And thus that even after a certain lapse of time did not pass into history, but continue at another level, in other ways and by other players? It is also possible that this topic still interests me because like everyone else I want to find a solution. I do not know. But I have composed another verse for the second time, and I have already tried to show my skills… in English. Here is the verse:

> We are divided by the "eleventh of nine"
> To "before" and "after," to "yours" and "mine".
> We are divided by the "eleventh of nine"
> To people who are bad, and who are fine.
> We are divided by the so-called human brain
> To extremists and humanists, again.
> All this rhetoric for me is like to threaten
> To divide parents from their own children.
> It means to me we want to separate air and water
> Forgetting that they can only exist together.
> There is not any weak ant and forceful lion,
> It is only our invention and our illusion.
> There is not any big difference among people,
> Our similarity is great, but our difference is simple.
> Through superficial diversity to intrinsic harmony-
> This is our way, our goal, our destiny.

By creating this verse I want to tell the following:

First, I am a man; afterwards, I am Azim. First, I am a rational being; afterwards, I am a scientist and a poet. First, I am a believer; afterwards, I am a Muslim. First, I am an inhabitant of the Earth; afterwards, I am a citizen of Tajikistan, and a resident of the US. First, I am a speaker; afterwards, I speak Tajik, English and Russian. All "firsts" are our similarities, unity, and intrinsic common roots; all "afterwards" are our diversity, differences, and superficial characteristics. There is double force of human reason, creative and destructive. Manhattan has been both constructed and destroyed by the human reason. I am for unity of diversities.

Finally, I want to say that we are teachers. If we continue to focus our activity on diversity and differences between people, cultures and religions, we can end up helping form a worldview among our students in which everyone differs from everyone else; in which everyone must be better and more powerful than the others and all ways and methods for achieving these goals are good. Right here it is possible that an incorrect interpretation of such ideas as "to be better," "to be stronger," "to show one's own power", etc., have appeared in the mind of a new generation, which might at times have grave consequences. If so, maybe on the fifth anniversary of those tragic events we should declare September 11th Reconsideration Day and talk with our students as much as possible about our equal origins (beginnings) and similarities, rather than differences? And through this activity might we make a valuable contribution to drawing people closer together? And finally, can we execute our mission—the mission of the most humane profession—teaching? I know, I have no right to state this on behalf of anyone else, but I believe that many other people hold such an opinion too. It is worth thinking about.

Learning to Be

Alexey Konobeev, PhD

– Russia –

Oh no, not this as well!–was my reaction to the phone call from the American Councils office, Moscow, in which they told me that I was to leave for the USA on JFDP program in a couple of months. I was standing at the doors of a large conference hall at the time, trying to calculate whether the university bus would be back in time to meet another group of participants, or I'd have to call a taxi. Being on the organizing board of an international conference is seldom an easy job, and even less easy when you are responsible for all transportation–among other things.

Another hard job I was thinking of at the time was my new position within the university–that of the dean of the preparatory faculty for international students. I had got promoted only a month before the phone call, and knew too well how much I still needed to learn to meet the challenges of the new position. Compared to my learning needs, the learning possibilities in the USA seemed moderate at best. And I had my reasons for thinking so. After five years of studying English at the university, one normally learned a lot about every English-speaking country, including geography, politics, history and culture in general. And how useful would a year in the USA be for my administrative job? And how many new things could I learn?

However, there was no going back. I won the grant and decided to go. Little did I imagine what a great learning experience I was going to have!

Rules of Thumb

When you deal with a foreign culture, no matter how close to your own it can be, you have to learn some basic rules of thumb. Many people are aware of this, but there is a huge difference between *knowing* and *feeling*. I first felt the importance of it when, at an orientation meeting in Moscow, all the JFDP fellows were asked to read the instructions and then to write their initials on every page as proof that we have read them and agree to follow them. Someone asked if we needed to sign every page, but no, mere initials were enough. This wouldn't have worked with any instructions in Russia; no one would trust just the initials. This was when I first felt that trust and responsibility were something I still needed to learn more about.

Trust and responsibility are always inseparable from safety. This was something I learned during orientation in Minneapolis. Many of us were fascinated by the alarm buttons on the premises of the University of Minnesota. They are not something you would normally see in a Russian university—mainly because they have been safe places for as long as I can remember. Therefore when I first saw the alarm buttons I felt something close to a shock. Even more shocking was the advice given to us on campus. "When you go for a walk in the city, always carry some cash on you. A twenty-dollar bill should work just fine. If someone mugs you, a twenty is enough for the robber and not something to grieve over for you. If you resist, or refuse to give the money, who knows, they may shoot you"—I was told. Uh-oh. That was not something I'd have expected at all! When I heard these words, I thought of the cash I had on me at the moment. Hey, I could afford being robbed ten timed and even then I'd have been only a couple of dollars short of another robbery! Life was... good?

I guess, for some of the JFDP fellows learning was harder than for me. Alongside with the customs and other "rules of thumb" they had to learn the language. I remember talking to another fellow in the university hall when she was telling me about a lecture she was once given in her home country. She said she felt really humiliated after that lecture, and then asked me: "How do I say this in English? Is it right to say it was a humiliating lecture?" Just as I was going to nod in agreement, we heard somebody say very pointedly: "HumiliatED! It's HUMILIATED, not humiliatING!" We turned to see who it was and noticed a lady from another former Soviet Union republic, who stamped her foot loudly and marched past us, apparently irritated by our illiteracy. That's how I learned another rule of thumb – do not interfere in someone else's conversation, even if you mean the best, unless you are ready to be judged as freely as you pass your own judgments.

Language alone can be a problem, but mingled with the foreign customs, it can lead to hilariously disastrous results. I think it was in early October. I was reading the university's newspaper when I saw an article about the national Coming-Out Day and the rally that was to take place next to the library building. I knew that my roommate came from a very conventional country, so I thought that a word of warning might come in handy as I knew he wasn't likely to be interested in listening to the speeches at the rally. So I turned to him and said casually:"You know, they are going to have a Coming-Out day rally near the library tomorrow. I don't know if you'll want to go and listen". "Really?"– was his reply–"I wonder why they have it so late in the year. In my country it usually happens in late August". You could have knocked me down with a straw. And I thought that his Moslem country was so traditionalist! "What do they do on this day?" – I asked. "Well, the usual stuff. They come to the schools they studied at, tell all about themselves, so that maybe some kids will want to grow up and follow in their footsteps. Don't they do it in your country?" "Hmm, not exactly…" I began saying, and then it dawned on me: "Ah, you mean HOMECOMING, not COMING OUT!" My roommate looked at me and asked: "What's the difference?"

Like it or not, but you have to be careful speaking a foreign language. At my host university I met a Russian girl who clearly preferred to spend time in the company of her compatriots, speaking Russian and picking up some sort of "anglicized" lingo from them. As part of that lingo, they often jokingly mispronounced some words. Once she was told about a cheap grocery store called "Fareway" and often did her shopping there. Pretty soon a colleague from our department asked her where she liked to do grocery shopping. "Far away, yes!" she said, unthinkingly repeating the lingo nickname of the store. I hope the colleague did not get offended by the answer.

Language and culture are fun to learn, but the greatest rule of thumb I learned in a non-fiction creative writing class. Frankly speaking, I felt very nervous and unsure about asking the professor to let me attend the class as I would be the only person there for whom English is not a native language. Besides, it was a master's level class, so it should be pretty high-level for me. Would I be able to understand? Would I be able to mingle with the aspiring writers? Or would I become a burden, a stranger listening to their stories? I e-mailed to the professor, and she agreed to let me come, but asked me to see her in her office prior to the class. From her biography I knew that she was an essayist and a poet who had published several books, and, to tell the truth, I had no idea what kind of person she would turn out to be. Would she be a wise elderly woman? Or would she be a stereotypical poetess, exquisite to the point of seeming sickly and airy?

It took me a while to find her office. When I opened the door, I saw a woman, who, for some reason, looked a bit Hindu. Maybe it was her olive skin, maybe her sari-like dress, maybe it was her long dark hair with light streaks in them that made this impression, but I immediately forgot everything the moment she smiled and spoke. She asked me to fully participate in the work of the class as many people in a non-fiction class write about personal things, and it might make them unwilling to share their feelings if there is someone who only listens to them speaking. Needless to say, I was more than happy to agree.

One of the students in the class was a guy in a wheelchair. Often it was hard for him to read long passages aloud as we were all required to do. In a Russian classroom he would have been asked to read shorter bits, or given easier assignments, but not in this class. It was then, after I was accepted in this class, after I saw that everybody was given an equal opportunity to participate, when I met other students from this class, some of whom had children and grandchildren, and others were just beginning their studies at the university, I felt that here learning was truly for everyone. This became the greatest rule of thumb for me, the one I enjoy and cherish most of all.

Rules of thumb are important only until you learn them. But as time goes by, the foreign country begins to seem less foreign to you. The excitement of living in a different culture subsides, and it is then when you begin to learn dozens of small things, without which you couldn't cope in everyday life.

Learning to Cope

The first thing that really puzzled me was having to select classes I wanted to attend from the university's catalogue. In Russia almost all classes are compulsory. They are pre-scheduled, you come to the university, find the number of your group in the time-table, and you know everything–what classes you are going to have on each day of the week, where they are going to be, at what time, etc. And even if you do not want to study a certain subject at this time or with this teacher (which is often the case), you have no choice. It's not easy to cope with the task of selecting classes from a long list and putting together your own time-table. I think I'd never have done it if it hadn't been for my adviser.

When I came into her office, she was ready to meet me, waiting with the huge volume of the catalogue. And although this middle-aged woman seemed a jolly nice person, the large volume looked intimidating. Little did I know that it was the moment when I met one of my best friends, whose presence made all things easy and cheerful. We started to choose the classes, began to exchange stories, and a quarter of an hour later we were chatting away, laughing out loud, so that some passers-by would peep into the office to see what was going on there. I still do not understand how it happened, but very soon in front of me lay a sheet of paper, written in my adviser's hand, with all the classes I could attend, their times and classroom locations. I did the selection myself for the next semester but I still keep the first schedule to remind me of the start of this friendship.

Getting to know the professors and the students was not hard. Very soon my creative writing teacher invited me to a cheese and wine party in her house so that I could meet some other professors. I remember the party well, but best of all I remember the moment when I turned to the hostess to say something and knocked down the mosquito net that was covering the doorway. I am sure this could become a good conversation piece, as it did with me and my roommate to whom I told the story the same evening. It may have somewhat destroyed the image of the "mysterious Russian soul", but it certainly made the guests smile to me more readily when they happened to meet me at the university afterwards.

For a while our greatest concern was accommodation. The one provided by the university was rather expensive for our stipends, so my roommate and I spent many hours trying to find an apartment. In the end we were lucky to find an unfurnished apartment in a good place at a very reasonable price. However, when you share the apartment, especially with someone from a different culture, there are many things to learn to get used to–different foods and cooking techniques, different life rhythms, different music tastes. I think it was more difficult for my roommate as he had never shared an apartment before, but both of us were ready to compromise, so everything went well except one mysterious thing.

Since the apartment was an unfurnished one, we had to buy many things. We haunted garage sales looking for furniture, but one decision was firm– dishes and cooking utensils had to be absolutely new. After all, just the two of us didn't need so much. So we soon bought everything, including a set of non-stick pans. And that's when the mystery appeared. Hardly had a week passed when my roommate told me that food began to stick to the pans. I looked at them–they were all scratched. But why? We had all sorts of wooden and plastic utensils, so we could be very careful. We ascribed the scratches to the low quality of the pans and bought a new set. Next week the story repeated. It was beginning to get a bit expensive, but we went shopping and bought yet another set. In the same evening my roommate offered to make some scrambled eggs with tomatoes. He always managed to make a great dish of them, so I gratefully accepted the offer. I was watching TV and I was almost dozing when a screech jerked me awake. It was my roommate, stirring the eggs with a fork–on the non-stick surface. Of course I said to him that we'd better do it with a plastic spatula or else the pans will be scratched again. He looked at me as if I was an idiot. "And how should I cut the eggs then, if I cannot use a knife?–he asked.

Another great learning experience for me was when I bought a car. Back in Russia I had never driven before, and I had big doubts if I'd ever be able to drive. So buying a car seemed a crazy thing to do. It seemed especially crazy because the buses in the city where I stayed were great, and with our university IDs we could ride them free. But I still bought a car. I did it because my adviser's husband advised me to do it and promised to teach me to drive.

It took me two months and two attempts to learn to drive and pass the driving test. But it changed my life no end. It was only when I got my driver's license I felt the true freedom of the USA. I was free to go wherever I liked. There are some wonderful parks around Ames, Iowa, as well as beautiful lakes and groves. The only disadvantage to them is that they are some way away from the city, and the city itself is nice but somewhat plain. But now–now I had access to everything. The cinemas in Des Moines, the picturesque old farmhouses around the city, the majestic Mississippi River – all were now within easy reach. But the best thing of all was that I could feel myself useful now. I could give rides to friends who needed to get to the airport, or wanted to be picked up somewhere, or just needed a ride from a nightclub. After years of teaching, when you know that you are needed somewhere, you get so used to this feeling that a lack of it suddenly leaves a gap in your life. But now I was feeling at home, and was ready to learn to love the country.

Learning to Love

In January I flew to Washington DC to the JFDP mid-year conference. Even in spite of it being the middle of winter, the city was impressive–more quiet than most capitals, serious-looking and with lots of free museums. There was very little time left for sightseeing as the conference last until 6 pm, but even so many fellows managed to roam the downtown in the evenings. On my last morning in Washington DC I went to the Capitol with a friend. This was very different from what going to the Russian Parliament in Moscow would have been like. The security was there, but they looked at us like at guests rather than like at would-be criminals. This was the dignity of many great men who had worked in the building that spread all around and made one respect the tradition, no matter how much one agreed or disagreed with the current politics. This was a feeling I loved.

Spring was settling in. The snow melted and a green haze was beginning to appear around trees and the grass was green on the campus lawn. Wind smelled of rains and the sky again became high and transparent. This was when I received an e-mail from the international students office, asking if I'd like to volunteer to make a presentation of my home country for kids in a local school. I grasped the opportunity – being an educator, I was naturally interested in seeing how children were taught in a different country. I spent several weeks searching the Internet for pictures of traditional sights and modern buildings, looking for samples of Russian folk music, planning the presentation, deciding on what would be most interesting for the children. Soon the day came when I, as well as some students from Spain, Germany, Japan, Korea and other countries, was driven to a school in a small town near Ames. I did not realize that I would have to make the same presentation three times, for different classes, but even though I spent most of the day at that school, I never ever felt tired or regretted it. I still remember the bright eyes of the children. I was talking about Russia, about its history, about the friendship that always existed between my country and the USA at most crucial moments in history. I was talking about people's love for their own country and of learning from other cultures to become richer. Later on I was sent the students' essays about my presentation, and I saw that I had my little share in teaching them to love their own country and see the world as a friendly place. As for me, from this trip I learned that children are basically the same everywhere, and I had a friend in the USA. He was a Russian guy who had moved to Los Angeles the previous summer, and at the time was staying in a long-term stay room in a hotel, working hard to earn his living. He used to phone me almost every evening, and we would spend a couple of hours chatting on the telephone. Given the two-hour time difference between California and Iowa, the phone call would begin at 11 pm my time and last till 1 in the morning. Anyway, he kept inviting me to come over, saying that it would be silly not to see Los Angelus and Hollywood. I kept counting the money that was left after paying all the bills and car insurance, but gradually I gave in to his reasoning. In mid-April I boarded the plane and flew to Los Angeles.

The contrast between Iowan spring and Californian all-year blooming beauty was striking. It is pointless to describe Hollywood and the beach in Malibu, as all I really saw was the sparkle of the ocean. It was only there that I truly felt the great diversity of the USA–and I knew that now I loved the country. On the plane back to Iowa I was thinking of how little it took me to start feeling at home in the USA, to learn to admire its diversity and mobility. But in spite of the spectacle of Californian palm trees, in spite of the museums of Washington DC, in spite of the wide beauty of the Mississippi; I felt that part of my heart now belonged in Iowa. I learned to love the hard-working farmers, who always waved their hands when I happened to drive by, I learned to feel grateful to the police officer who, after I had a flat tire on the highway, stopped and helped me to replace the wheel, I learned to need the quiet parks and lakes, and I even learned to put up with the white dust on the roads. Flying to Iowa now felt like homecoming.

But there was little time left. June came, and with it came the fuss of getting ready for my birthday and also for returning to Russia. In Russia, when you have a birthday, you usually go out with friends, or have dinner together, or, if you prefer, have dinner with your family. Imagine how surprised I was when I learned that my friends – that is, my adviser and her husband, and also some other people I met in Iowa, were going to make a birthday dinner for me! I was grateful not so much because they went to the trouble of buying food, cooking and making presents, but because it meant that I also belonged there. And although I still had about three weeks left before my return flight to Russia, it felt like a farewell dinner, with the time to say good-bye approaching fast.

I remember many things about this year. I remember studying with other students, I remember long talks with professors, when I not only listened, but had something to say about the subjects they taught, and they were interested in hearing a word from the other side of the ocean. I remember a late flower that I saw near a bus stop in early November, a time when days are short and gray in my part of Russia. I remember the conferences I went to and the presentations I made there. I remember assisting in teaching a few classes. I remember the tears in my adviser's eyes when I was saying good-bye to her before boarding the plane. I remember the two hundred dollars that I saved for the return flight – it wasn't much, but I pulled through, since my tickets were covered by the grant. And most clearly I remember the lessons that this stay in the USA taught me—the rules of thumb, the lessons that taught me to cope with all sorts of situations, and the great lessons of love that the country taught me. When I returned to Russia I realized how much I had learned over that year. That was much more than I actually dreamt. And although not all of this knowledge is directly applicable to my administrative job, I still learned to be. To be in a different culture, to be Russian and to be proud of it, to be ever respectful of other cultures and to be a different person. Altogether, I think this was a great learning experience in more than one way.

Azerbaijani Music at Indiana University

Aida Huseynova, PhD

– Azerbaijan –

Rudyard Kipling would probably have never written his sacramental "East is East, and West is West, and never the twain shall meet" if he had got a chance to see what was happening in spring 2002 in one of the halls at the Indiana University School of Music, Bloomington. Twice a week, a choir of IU students known as the International Vocal Ensemble (IVE) together with its Artistic Director, Dr. Mary Goetze and the author of this essay were singing Azerbaijani folk songs, perfectly rendering all peculiarities of Azerbaijani music and language. On April 21, accompanied by Chingiz Sadikhov, outstanding Azerbaijani pianist now living in the United States, IVE performed these songs along with Chinese, Yugoslavian and Russian pieces at its spring concert. On April 19, 2002 maestro Sadikhov also gave a solo recital on Azerbaijani music.

Challenge of Working with a Choir

I have never worked with a choir before coming to America. In Azerbaijan State Conservatory which I graduated from in 1987 I studied piano and musicology. The topic of my doctoral dissertation that I defended at the Saint Petersburg Conservatory in 1992 was far from choral music as well–I wrote about the legacy of Azerbaijani composer Muslim Magomayev, one of the founders of art music tradition in the country. My only experience in choral music dated to my teenage when I was singing in a choir as a pupil of public music school. I clearly remember that I enjoyed that a lot. However, singing in a choir and teaching a choir are completely different tasks! Another challenge was that I had never performed Azerbaijani folk songs in academic context. Apparently, I had known many of them, since I grew up in Azerbaijan, in the atmosphere of folk songs and dances, as well as the richest genre of Azerbaijani traditional music called mugham included in 2003 in UNESCO's List of Masterpieces of Oral and Intangible Heritage of Humanity. However, I never thought that one day Azerbaijani folk songs would be placed in a focus of my professional activities. This is what happened to me while in the United

States. Paradoxical observation–America helped me to understand deeper the cultural and musical legacy of my native country.

International Vocal Ensemble

This exciting project would have never been carried out but for Dr. Mary Goetze, Professor of Music, Chair of the Music in General Studies Department, founder and director of IVE. It's amazing how carefully this wonderful musician–composer, author, arranger and conductor – is exploring diverse music traditions all over the world passing along to young generations not only her gained knowledge but also deepest respect for different cultures and music outside the Western world. Began in 1995, IVE, "a unique and uniquely powerful campus bastion of cross-cultural communication" (Bloomington Independent, November 22, 2001) so far had learned and performed music from South Africa, Israel, Russia, Turkey, Argentina, Brazil, Iran, Kyrgyzstan and Tibet. The main concept of the choir set by Dr. Goetze is to emulate folk models by singing in the native language and re-creating music and movement as they come from the tradition. For this reason, Dr. Goetze invites representatives of the native cultures whom she calls "informants" to participate in the rehearsal process and assist in re-creating the musical model. Besides, "informants" are supposed to provide information about the culture and the country these songs come from. This was a responsible and honorable role that I enjoyed in spring 2002 along with musicians from Yugoslavia, Chine and Russia.

Indiana University: Home of Diversity

The idea to perform Azerbaijani music in IU was not spontaneous. For the last decade the Bloomington community has had many opportunities to expose to Azerbaijani music–due to the tremendous efforts of Dr. Shahyar Daneshgar, IU Research Associate as well as performances of guest artists from Azerbaijan such as the incredible mugham performer, winner of the 1999 UNESCO International music prize Alim Gasimov. Since 2000, IU faculty members, including Professor of Voice, Dr. James McDonald and coach accompanist, Ruth Ann McDonald, as well as Associate Professor of Saxophone and Jazz Studies Dr. Thomas Walsh, have been visiting Azerbaijan, giving master classes and performing at Baku Music Academy, country's major music school. As a tribute to Azerbaijani colleagues, Thomas Walsh included a composition Nostalgy by Azerbaijani jazz musician Vagif Sadikhov in his CD "New Life" released in 2002. All these links have not been occasional. Indiana University has a nationwide reputation of being a home for an extraordinarily diverse population of people from many backgrounds, many countries, many cultures and many religions. And, naturally, the idea of cultural diversity and appreciation of various cultural and musical traditions remains as one of the milestones of Bloomington community. One of the most splendid celebrations of Novruz, the holiday of vernal equinox in many Central Asian cultures, happens in Indiana University every March. I myself participated in the two of them, in 2000 and 2002 where performed Azerbaijani music on the piano and performed traditional dances. Words of deepest appreciation and gratitude should be addressed to Indiana University's Inner Asian and Uralic National Resource Center (IAUNRC) and its Director, Professor William Fierman, one of the country's leading experts on Central Asia. Most of exciting cultural events in the Indiana University related to Central Asian region and, without exception, all projects described in this essay, have become possible due to kind support of IAUNRC and Dr. Fierman.

Bloomington-Baku

When I first met Dr. Goetze in February 2000 she had already been intrigued with the music tradition of Azerbaijan. In June 2000 Dr. Goetze included Azerbaijani songs in the program of the Multicultural Music Education seminar in Bloomington and two months later she herself came to Baku. I will never forget those wonderful days when Dr. Goetze, ignoring unusual heat and various everyday complexities, met Azerbaijani colleagues, listened to children choirs and recorded music excerpts. "I was amazed to learn of the lively musical tradition of Azerbaijan—mugham, classical music and, of course, the way jazz has been fused with traditional melodic material," she said. "I wanted my students to be aware of this country and its musical traditions." That's why when knowing about my upcoming one-year residence in Bloomington as a JFDP fellow; she immediately came to the conclusion: IVE would be learning Azerbaijani folk songs and I would be serving as "informant." To create "a real Azerbaijani spirit" we involved Chingiz Sadikhov in our project. His fantastic ability to improvise Azerbaijani music on piano and impeccable artistic taste have mesmerized many generations of music lovers in Azerbaijan and abroad. He was known as an accompanist working with Azerbaijan's many star vocalists, such as Rashid Behbudov, Muslim Magomayev and others. In January 2002 I met maestro Sadikhov in San Francisco where he had been in residence since 1994 and discussed all aspects of our project. We agreed that he would arrive in Bloomington one week prior to the concert and join the IVE rehearsals.

Rehearsal Process

Songs chosen to be learned undoubtedly are among the most favorites in Azerbaijan: "Bari Bakh" (arranged by Rauf Babayev) which captivated Dr. Goetze since she had heard it in Baku when performed by the famous children's group of the same name, "Ay Gulabatin" (arranged by Ramiz Mustafayev) remarkable with its expressive harmonic texture and "Gul Achdi" (arranged by Jahangir Jahangirov) which would provide variety and a bit of melancholic feeling. The days of rehearsals in IU School of Music Sweeney Hall remain among sweetest memories of my American trip. It was fascinating how students grasped the general idea of melodies and rhythms fairly quickly. Katherine Domingo, Assistant Director, was not surprised with that at all. "All the songs are tuneful, rhythmic and a lot of fun to sing," she said. "I think these songs will continue to live in us after this semester ends." It was much more difficult to memorize and achieve exact pronunciation of the text. "This is probably the most challenging aspect because the vowel sounds are unfamiliar", admitted Dr. Goetze. "Original script has been transcribed into a modified form of International Phonetic Alphabet, but we rely heavily on Aida`s modeling of the phonemes in order to pronounce the words to the songs." And one of the jolliest aspects of our rehearsals was learning some traditional Azerbaijani dance movements–students were imitating them very smoothly and with zest.

Culture via Music

Music is admitted to be among the most effective vehicles helping to understand the culture. "The songs we learn reveal many things about the culture–light-hearted, fun and praising the beauty of the natural surroundings", Katherine said. My role as an "informant" was not only to provide musical knowledge but also to acquaint students with the culture from which the music comes. Dr. Goetze considers it an important part of the rehearsal process. We watched slides and video excerpts she recorded in Baku: Maiden's Tower, Nizami Museum, Market street, kids at play, a refugee beggar... Almost all the pictures were of current life in Baku... It was an indescribable pleasure to answer the students` numerous questions that revealed their sincere interest for the country, its history and lifestyle, values and customs. Young Americans were getting to know Azerbaijan. And this was, of course, the main value of our project.

Success

Finally, the Big Day had come! To say that our concert was complete success is to say nothing. As a member of the choir and accompanist in one of the songs, I experienced all emotional nuances that musicians on stage feel during and after a successful performance. There is a certain point familiar to each and every musician when you become aware of whether or not you have accomplished your goals. I had got this feeling – a bit forgotten, since during last years I was mostly a scholar rather than a performer on stage. Gorgeous Auer Hall of IU School of Music was filled with applauses and signs of admiration addressed to Dr. Mary Goetze, students that worked hard and achieved a lot, and maestro Chingiz Sadikhov who incorporated his incredible mastery in the success of the performance. During next days we continued to enjoy words of appreciation from people around, local newspapers and one more source that I still consider the most special. As a teaching assistant in Dr. Goetze's The Live Musical Experience class, I was responsible for grading written assignments. After the concert Dr. Goetze asked the students to share their impressions of the event. I still keep these precious manuscripts, filled with love and appreciation. Here are some quotes: "I really loved music from Azerbaijan. The songs express beauty, nature and love. They had the most beautiful piano parts played by the Maestro. His skill as a pianist is beyond comprehension. Each note is played with strong dynamics. He also has such a wonderful timbre and vibrato when he sings. It was an honor to hear him. What a treat" (Amy Birnbaum). "I loved Azerbaijani part of the concert. Chingiz Sadikhov`s use of thrills was remarkable. The improvisation, which is a key element in Azerbaijani music, was remarkable too. Thirdly, the man is an entertainer. As we have seen, the visual and performance aspect of music is an important element; his (seemingly impromptu) encore was spectacular. He knows how to make a performance look good as well as sound great" (Bill Hogan). "I most enjoyed the music of Azerbaijan, with Chingiz Sadikhov`s performance. This was because of the strong, rhythmic beats of "Bari Bakh," the beautiful melody of Chinghiz`s piano playing, and the exquisite dynamic changes from one song to the next. Excellent" (Caroline Lopushinsky).

Post Script

Soon after the concert I got one more chance to teach Azerbaijani songs at Indiana University–now to college and university teachers from all over the world. Dr. Goetze invited me to be a guest musician at the Workshop on Multicultural Music Education to be held in Bloomington in June 2002. My role was similar and different from what I have already done with IVE. My duties were the same–teaching songs and providing the information on Azerbaijani culture. Meanwhile, time format was different–we had to learn two songs in three days, since all the participants were supposed to take this experience to their home schools. This was the most exciting outcome of the project–to know that even after my return to Azerbaijan, the songs of my land would be performed in American classrooms. If someone had told me about this possibility a year ago, I would have considered it a bold dream. I didn't know at that time that soon after my return I would get an invitation to participate in the Global Voices project, the creative brainchild of Dr. Mary Goetze and Jay Fern. They have been working on this project for almost 10 years already producing audio and video materials related to the music of Hungary and Swazi from Africa. A series of 6 DVDs with 24 songs was produced for classroom instruction in Grades 1-6 and contained songs from fifteen countries, including Azerbaijan, Brazil, Ghana, Holland, India, Ireland, Japan, Korea, Mexico, New Zealand, Norway, South Africa, Philippines and Zimbabwe. Macmillan and McGraw Hill, well known education publisher in the United States has included this project in their series Spotlight on Music. Two Azerbaijani songs chosen for the project, "Jip Jip Jujalarim" by Gambar Huseynli and folk song "Bari Bakh" (again!) have been presented the same way we did in Indiana–the DVDs feature not only performances of the songs but also include teaching materials helping to learn melodies and lyrics as well as provide comprehensive cultural context. Indeed, it is magic that now, somewhere, say, in Texas or Michigan young Americans are singing favorite songs of my land, and their voices are alternating with voices of young Azerbaijanis, although coming from thousands miles away.

Rudyard Kipling's era is behind. Apparently, "East is East and West is West", however," the twain is meeting" over and over, and it is due to us, our views and efforts where and how this meeting occurs. It is an axiom that music is probably the most effective way to build bridges of tolerance and understanding. After American experience, these words have a particular value for me. I am grateful to Junior Faculty Development Program, I am grateful to America and all my friends and colleagues at Indiana University, as well as Columbia University, Ohio State University, Purdue University, University of Madison, Wisconsin, and University of Chicago where I gave presentations and participated in conferences. Dr. Mary Goetze and Dr. William Fierman will forever remain among the dearest people in my life–they not only supported my modest efforts to introduce music of my country in America, but also helped me understand many important things about music and life. In summer 2005, together with Dr. Goetze we traveled to Kyrgyzstan where collected folk melodies and recorded pictures of traditional culture and life. Nowadays, I am teaching History of American jazz in my home institution, Baku Music Academy. All these are little yet precious contributions to make our world smaller, safer and happier. When music sounds, no violence is going to happen. When nations share their music heritage they are not alien anymore.

Finding Similarity in Diversity

Natalia Kuznetsova, PhD

– Russia –

It is quite a demanding task to write about past events because our memory sorts out things that happened with us according to special emotional laws of love, courage and forgiveness, understanding and frustration, losses and challenge. My American year that happened in 2000/2001 is colored with a sparkling spectrum of all these feelings and even after five years that passed since my return to Russia I am not able to realize all consequences of my staying there. Before my coming to the USA I had knowledge about this country that I got at school and University but it was abstract and distant like Latin. After spending a year in the USA, thanks to people whom I got to know in Pittsburgh State University–Bob Donnorumo, my supervisors Mary Briscoe and Arthur Erbe, Linnea Alison and many others, I became emotionally involved in its life and culture and since that time I feel strong connections and gratitude toward this country.

A long-lasting impact of the American culture was so strong that everybody who spent a year in the USA as a JFDP fellow could say that subtle changes in his/her character, attitudes and believes are still going on and this is the object of analysis in my essay on similarities and diversity that we all met there.

I want to dwell upon some assumptions concerning my staying in the USA for the sake of truth and objectivity of my memories. When you write out things you have a good chance to keep them with you and that is why I am writing this essay. So, my assumptions are the following: first of all, people who came to the USA for a year as JFDP fellows were similar and different at the same time. Second, the country where they came had much in common with their own countries and was different from them. Finally, JFDP fellows could find and found similar and different things in the USA to bring them home. The overwhelming diversity of American life influenced our souls and minds and changed us all forever and this needs to be discussed!

First, when more than one hundred people came to the USA in 2000, they had something that united them all, one common feature–they went through a very strict competition of scientific projects and interviews and they could be proud of themselves because it was a professional achievement for all of them to get JFDP scholarships. We attained our common goal differently. Some of us were America's first choice – they wrote their statements of purpose and successfully came through the interview after the first attempt. As for me I applied for this program four times constantly learning from my mistakes and finally made it. I could remember many people of different age, from different parts and regions of former Soviet Union and of different professional background in our group when we arrived to Delaware for our orientation. The majority was young people but some of us were middle-aged ones. My educational background was quite typical and could illustrate global changes that were going on after the period of transition in Russia.

I was born in Russia, spent my childhood in a small provincial town Borovichi not far from Novgorod the Great and St. Petersburg and when I came to America I was 42 years old. I started to learn English when I was eight years old in 1966. My first and *main* teacher of English was Alexandra Pavlovna Kudryavtseva who made me feel permanent astonishment and later, love toward the secrets and logic of the English language. She was a skilled and devoted teacher and her lessons became intellectual festivals for her pupils combining hard work with rare inspirations and victories. I can not say that the methods she tried were directly connected with the dominating nowadays communicative approach, but what I remember well was her faith in us. We strongly believed that it was possible to learn a foreign language and it was necessary to learn English to become a smart person. Another school teacher–Tatyana Ivanovna Dorenko, a young intellectual after St. Petersburg University taught me to love Russian and Foreign Literature. She delivered an extra-curriculum course in Foreign Literature for the students of the ninth and tenth grade studying both classical and modern works. It was the act of courage and intellectual freedom at that time and she gave us the opportunity to think and speak about universal problems touched by first-rank foreign writers. We did not understand much but it was a hint on another life and another mentality and values. After our reading "The Catcher in the Rye" by Salinger some parents got infuriated when we started asking questions, some tried to answer dwelling on them for the first time from another point of view. The most influential and memorable thing about my school years was that strange mixture of intellectual freedom, slight dissension for the sake of spiritual maturation and the ability to read as much as I wanted. It was the logical choice for me to enter the Faculty of Foreign Languages at Novgorod

45

State Pedagogical Institute in 1975, to write my PhD (candidate of science dissertation) on Nathaniel Hawthorne's early tales in 1991, to defend it in St. Petersburg Pedagogical University in 1995 and to continue working on my doctoral dissertation studying the change of values in American novels of Vladimir Nabokov. Wide range of intellectual interests and my focusing on values that modify human behavior and choices made me to apply for different scientific programs. In 1996 I spent a month in Hertfordshire University in England under the grant of the British Academy of Science and worked out the curriculum on bilingual course in approaches to teaching foreign languages. Coming to America for a year to work in the libraries on American Literature matters was a precious gift which value I fully recognized and persistently tried to prove my right to get it.

All people who arrived to Delaware and lately came to different Universities around the USA had one more common feature—they were educators and more or less they could apply the motto of the medieval scholar and monk the Venerable Bede who lived from 673 to 735 A.D. to their occupation and lives. He wrote: "All my life I like reading, writing and teaching most of all". The degree of liking these things was different among us JFDP fellows, but we all were eager to learn something new from the American academic culture. I enjoyed the opportunity to choose totally new courses which I could attend in Pittsburgh University. I worked as a teacher of English as a Foreign Language and Foreign Literature at the Faculty of Educational Science and Psychology in Novgorod State University and I took "Literature and Psychoanalysis", "Short Story in the Context" for the honors students and the advanced course in Methods of teaching English as a Foreign Language. I got acquainted with the American way of teaching and learning because I performed two roles at the same time: I read a lot to prepare for the classes as a student and sometimes I participated in discussions presenting my views as a teacher. It was challenging and gave me a push to learn how to use IT in my studies, how to write papers, how to work due deadlines and so many other things.

Our expectations from the year in America were different and now I may say that we wanted to explore not only the American academic life but American way of life and culture as well. And JFD Program was a great chance to see and feel everything from inside and "take it or leave it". All the year round we watched American TV shows and films, tried to speak with American accent, read American newspapers and magazines, flew by American airplanes to different American airports and changed to make connections, ate American food and celebrated American holidays in different American cities and towns. Besides, I followed the first election company of the President

Bush and discussed it with my American colleagues, I participated in the scientific conferences that took place in Las Vegas and in Washington, DC, I celebrated Halloween, Thanksgiving Day, Christmas and the Independence Day, I traveled to Miami for my spring vacation, I stood frozen with delight and admiration staring at beautiful horses taken from 15 states to Celebration of a Horse in a Leaganeer Natural Reserve and so on and so forth. The cultural experience was so multifaceted that could hardly be described rationally. But in the terms of similarity and diversity my American cultural experience could be described as the overwhelming diversity of everything and I needed time to absorb all its newness first of all and then I needed distance to sort out its attractions. This process is still going on and the images of American culture are constantly emerging in my every day life and I gladly recognize them in my present Russian environment like well known people not always friends but acquaintances from other life. An annual fragment of American culture and life came through my heart and found a considerable place there – they became the part of me forever and I want to say "Thank you, America", for sharing your everyday trifles and ever-lasting treasures with me. You gave my friends and me the opportunity to live them through and realize our difference and likeness.

My second assumption about the similarity and difference between our countries was proven from my first steps in America. First, like everywhere, I had to find the place to live and buy food, try the ways of transportation to the University, organize my schedule, explore the access to the Internet and libraries, learn how to use the ATM machines, etc. But all these things shared by millions in the world certainly had American shape and way and I had to adjust to them. In Russia I had an old two-room flat where I lived for all my life and in America I had to learn a lot about the process of renting apartment that impressed me with its clear legal formulas of rights and duties for both sides – for me as a renter and for my landlord. To my surprise it was written there that I had the right to put a Christmas tree in my room but it was my duty to ask my landlord to take it away from my room after Christmas. I accepted this rule gladly.

What I like about domestic ways in the US was a choice to live wherever I wanted according to my preferences. I tried many places in different parts of Pittsburgh and rented a beautiful quiet one bedroom apartment ten minutes walk from the Cathedral of Learning in Bayard Street. It was an apartment without furniture and I visited a Good Will shop to buy some necessary things such as plates, spoons, forks, cups for the House warming party where my guests brought a TV set, a table and two arm-chairs with them. These pieces were left by the former fellows and they helped me to furnish my dwelling. My guests also gave me touching presents to make me to feel at home in my apartment – flowers, pictures, table cloth, flower pots, candles and a small carpet. This kindness and support helped me to overcome my homesickness and start my work.

Describing my study and work in Pittsburgh University in 2000/2001 I want to cite an extract from Brian Boyd's book "Vladimir Nabokov. American Years" where he wrote about Nabokov's perception of the American academic culture in Wellesley College. These words are so close to my mind and they reflect the same feelings that I completely share with Nabokov remembering my lessons in the Cathedral of Learning. "Nabokov fell in love with Wellesley at once... After some years he pointed out that teachers at Wellesley College were mainly concerned about science and students' well being and not about their prestige and position. This attitude towards students he treated as the typical manifestation of the American kindness, and he thought of the free access to the books on the library shelves as the best evidence of the American openness." This was the main difference between Russian libraries and American ones that appealed to my heart and mind. I understand all technical and financial difficulties of such free access to books for the students and teachers but I treat the time I spent in Pittsburgh University library as the most memorable one. Like other readers I could stay there till 0100 a.m. (if I had physical ability to do so) and a special bus would take me directly to my house. The openness of the American culture and science to other people who want to spend their time and effort to share and take it was the most impressing feature and I want to praise this openness here.

Like everywhere in the world in Russia people value such personal qualities as kindness, reliability, intelligence, professionalism, politeness. In America I met with some more values that I brought with me back to my native country. First, this is a way of feeling and doing things. I could feel compassion towards the disabled but only after the American experience of buying things in Good Will shops with disabled people working where as shop-assistants I graduated from the correspondent Harmony Project courses in writing applications for grants for the civic NGOs and started to write grant applications for those who are not able to do this. I started to support people with practical doings. In 2001 just after my return to Russia I worked with the Canadian expert for the giving 3HHH grant from Rotary club for starting a joint co-learning of disabled and healthy children. Now I help to write grant applications in the sphere of age concern and in 2006 I got the grant from the Council of Ministers of Northern Countries for the joint social work of widows of war and my students who work as volunteers. Second, I became more attentive and rational in realization of my ideas because I started to value time and effort. In May, 2005 I met the former president of NASULGC Peter Magrath who came to Novgorod State University as the head of Saltsburg Seminar expert team and he told me about the stable interest in the USA to the Russian language and culture. He also advised me to think about teaching Russian as a Foreign Language and Russian Culture in America. I found this idea very interesting because I had my own personal experience of learning and teaching English as a foreign language and being a Russian native speaker I could imagine all linguistic difficulties that my students could face learning Russian. I might use my English as the language of instruction to explain to them Russian cultural realms. I seriously took his advice and studied methods of teaching Russian as a Foreign Language at Moscow State University (world famous for its communicative approach) and got a diploma in June, 2006. Third, I became more tolerant to diversity of other people and try to explain these differences taking into consideration ethnical, educational and social background. It helps me to take people and things as they are, don't cherish illusions and do what depends on me to change the world for the better. From my American experience I teach students to take responsibility for their own lives and not to be afraid of changes and challenges.

Finally, I have discussed my last assumption about possibilities, initiatives and directions for further development that everyone could notice in America and later could realize in his/her own country. I want to conclude my essay with a Latin saying, that seemed abstract to me when I was a child but became clear and meaningful later: *Cives nati, cives facti.* In ancient times there were people who were born Roman citizens who enjoyed all rights, they were called *cives nati.* People who got the Roman citizenship for some outstanding deeds or for some other reasons were called *cives facti,* and usually their rights were limited in comparison with the first group. But that was so in ancient Rome and as time passed we may interpret our status differently. We are all *cives nati* on our planet Earth, and we have to do our best to become *cives de-facto et de-iure* with the right and duty to improve our world.

Belated Maturation: My American Experience

Mirjana Bobic, PhD

– Serbia –

It was August, 1ˢᵗ 2005 when I received the announcement of Junior Faculty Development Program, the fellowship of American Councils, organization of Bureau of Educational and Cultural Affairs of State Department. It was stated that the purpose of the grant was improving professional skills and scientific knowledge of teachers and trainees from universities in transitional countries of Eastern Europe and Euro Asia, by offering them an opportunity to spend a semester long time (5 months) at American universities.

I somehow wasn't completely satisfied with myself, although I had had all the reasons of this world to be happy and fulfilled. I had a good job and was respected in society. I was pretty well off in comparison to other parts of Serbian population in transition. But first and foremost, I was beloved wife and mother of two gorgeous daughters. I and my family were the "winners" in post socialistic transition, due to the fact that we were the part of the stratum of elites (intellectuals). And as is well known, modernization can't be furthered on without educated persons, so called meritocracy. My husband is a mechanical engineer, working in a nationally famous enterprise that builds bridges. I am assistant professor at one of the most prestigious faculties (schools) of Belgrade University, which is the leading institution in Serbia and at the Balkans.

My faculty (school) of Philosophy as well as the University of Belgrade commenced the reforms of educational process according to the recommendations of European Union (The Bologna process). Department of Sociology, were I teach, has been one out of "frontrunners" of the transformation of higher education. My colleagues and I initiated changes in teaching process, through improvements of: structure of required and elective courses, introducing the system of credits (points) per year, etc. We have had plenty of debates and dilemmas on the goals, direction and pace of the reform. My main objection was that we can't make a progress unless we observe the issues in more developed countries and universities. We can't change things from within ourselves, by guessing and wondering… To my opinion, it was much more reasonable to observe *in vivo* colleagues from more advanced educational systems. "The teachers ought to be taught" as the Latin saying poses.

Application For US Grant: What I Really Wanted

When I submitted my application for JFDP, I actually knew exactly what I wanted. I wished to gain some insight into teaching process in America, having in mind that their system is more efficient as well as better incorporated to the demands of job market. I also had some previous information that they offer students learning skills and knowledge that is more applicable, that the educational system is pragmatic, flexible, opened up for permanent improvements and adaptations to the economy. Besides that, the learner centered classrooms is something what me and my faculty were trying to introduce in our practice, as well as to make students take more active roles in the whole process. I didn't realize exactly how I could mobilize my students to come prepared for the classes, so that we can discuss and perform workshops and exchange of opinions instead of my pure oral lecturing.

So, when I showed up at the interview at the office of American Councils in Belgrade, after I had previously passed the first step of the selection process, I explained my motivation to travel to US, exactly as I described it above, as a pure professional one. Of course, as a sociologist I also had a strong incentive to observe American style of everyday life, their families, institutions, civil life. From my early childhood, when I started learning English language with my private tutor, I wanted to visit America, "the land of promise", as we were used to call it. I used to argue with my parents, who were socialized to adore Russia, while I always preferred America. And I "did have a dream" to quote Martin Luther King to visit that great land one day. And I thought this was a chance for my dreams come true!

Arrival to America in *January*: A Metaphor of a New Beginning

After a short preparatory period in Belgrade, I with my eight colleagues from universities in Serbia and Montenegro departed to America. In Washington DC, we joined the rest of fellows from Balkan states and Euro Asia to form a large group of some seventy participants. It was so heterogeneous community of teachers and instructors, best specimen and distinguished intellectuals in their home countries. The large group was, however, composed of different generations, cultures, socioeconomic and educational backgrounds, religious, ethnic and other affiliations. We were to spend several days attending a pre-departure conference at DC in a very luxurious hotel.

It soon became obvious that there were serious differences among the fellows from Balkan states (Serbia and Montenegro, Croatia, Bosnia and Herzegovina) and the rest of them from Eurasia. Due to inequalities of our social milieu at home, pace and tempo of post communist economic reforms, present living standards, life (and world) experiences and consequently, motivations and expectations from this visit and stay in the USA. According to my perceptions, based on observation of comments and behaviors of fellows during the sessions and at informal occasions at coffee and lunch breaks, many of the colleagues that stem from less developed transitional countries came to America, in an attempt to find the strategy of raising their living conditions, to try to catch as much opportunities as is possible in order to escape from hardships of their everyday lives in their countries of origin.

Despite that, most of us from South Europe, have already traveled abroad a lot, many of us were visiting lecturers throughout the Europe. Two of us from the group have already been in the USA. Like me, all of us were primarily focused on professional achievements: either on completing PhD thesis or upgrading knowledge and teaching skills (my case). As we arrived at America with a lot of savings brought from home, we started creating the itineraries, for this was also the unique opportunity to travel and explore this great and wonderful country. And a chance to meet each other at various locations, such as New York City, Las Vegas, Colorado, Hollywood, Florida, and Chicago.

Next Step: Staying All Alone By Myself

After a five-day period together at DC, we were separated in order to travel to different Universities all over America. I had a flight to Portland, Maine, as a visiting faculty at Muskie School of Public Service, University of Southern Maine. I found myself completely alone after a very long time, actually for the first time ever since I was a small child. Namely, I got married very young, at the age of 23, right from my parents' home and went to live with my husband and his parents. I was never on my own, particularly not so far away from my home and for such a long time. My parents sent me to London for 1 month during summer, in order to improve my English speaking skills, but it was some 30 years ago and I traveled with one of my relatives. In England we joined up a group of many other students from my country.

This time I was not a young student anymore. Besides that, I was coming from the country that had gained a very disadvantaged political position in the world due to the bad image created during the 1990s. Former political leadership and elites that were thrown away in a democratic procedure, through elections in 2000, pursued several wars in Balkans, producing that many foreign citizens treated Serbs as killers, "butchers," uncivilized, and wild. It wasn't an easy task to carry such a load on one's shoulders and try to convince people that that wasn't true. That all Serbs are not alike and I am a different Serb. And, that the impressions about common Serbs are actually pure prejudices. During all the unhappy years of 1990s, I often felt so ashamed to be a citizen of Serbia. I knew that there were a lot of misunderstandings on the part of international community related to the situation at my home country, but anyway, it wasn't so simple to identify yourself with your country.

Soon I realized that there was no reason for me to worry because my new American colleagues and friends didn't show any hostility towards me. Quite contrary, they showed much more understanding and happened to be better informed about the recent events and earlier history than I could have expected! They actually helped me to start to feel better in my own skin and become much more proud of my own origins. I have seen the American flags at every corner of the town, at private properties, at the swimming pool, at public buildings and it has shown to be an incentive for me to start appreciating my national symbols much more. And, finally I became fully aware of the fact that you can't like some other culture and accept it unless you don't know: who you are, what are your origins, if you do not love your home and your parents first and foremost.

Quite frankly, I have to admit that I actually grew up in my late 40ties. America helped me to become a personality instead of a being pure individual!! I remembered the words of famous social psychologist Erich Fromm saying that *some people die before they are born as persons*. I think I managed to become a person thanks to America! The very place of my stay, Portland, Maine, was really wonderful. Small, nice town, with a lot of parks, at the coast of Atlantic Ocean, with so frank citizens, smiling at you and always ready to help. My American colleagues were kind and supportive, too, my advisor, particularly. Unlike the rest of my colleagues from Serbia and other JFDP fellows, I didn't face the challenges of a culture of individualism. On the contrary, I felt quite comfortable to be left on my own. I preferred to wonder dawn the streets and go for a long walks. I made my everyday and weekly plans and schedules for reading, writing, meetings with new colleagues and friends, as well as recreation (I used to go to swimming pool twice a week). I enjoyed my classes, took part in discussions with American students and their instructors. Although it wasn't required to, I was utmost honored when I was asked to make three presentations in classes. The topics were the following: 1) the position of women in Serbian society in transition; 2) qualitative methodology in investigation of marriage patterns in Serbia; 3) refugees and internally displaced persons in Serbia.

And what's the most important: I had a lot of time to reflect on myself, my dilemmas and ways to overtake them. The first one, personal was resolved as I had described earlier on these pages. The second one—as to my future teaching style and transformation from a teacher centered to a learner centered model was also on the way to be successfully accomplished due to my active participation in American classrooms. The third one referred to my professional research perspectives. It had also been resolved thanks to my stay at Muskie School of Public Service, and through intensive professional conversations I had conducted with my advisor, Dahlia Lynn and the dean of the School, Bill Foster. Those are the two persons I am mostly grateful to for helping me realize how to redirect my future professional orientation. I made up my mind to focus to more practical and public policy issues. With the goal to try to deploy my knowledge to improve the lives of my countrymen and raise the standards in everyday life through: health service, social protection, transformation of gender relations, and familial interactions.

Conclusive Remarks: Ready to Start Over at Home

And finally, after five months of stay in America, my family as well as my mother and brother were all thrilled to see me back. They missed me so much, as much as I missed them. It wasn't easy to be separated from them for such a long time. But it looked as if I had to go far away in order to find the way to restructure and recombine my personality and my biography. "You are completely different person," they admitted after a while. "You have changed in such a positive way," my friends and relatives agreed, too.

Yes, I feel that too. Thank you America! At the first place and thanks to myself for not loosing hope and being brave to make such a great adventure.

Far From Ukraine: Looking Back on a Year Spent in America

Valentyna Arkhelyuk, PhD

–Ukraine –

The things that have happened to me in the last couple of years are different than anything I ever would have expected. If anybody had told me that I'd receive the grant for visiting the USA, I could not have imagined it. First, because I was not sure that I could participate in the 'junior' Faculty Development Program (JFDP): I was 40 when I applied. Second, I was not sure I could be away from my family for a long time (a lovely husband and two gorgeous kids-teenagers: son & daughter).

I took a train to Chernivtsi (Ukraine) after my interview in Kiev. The next morning when I started my work at Chernivtsi National University (CNU) I got a call from the ACTR/ACCELS office in Kiev with the words: "Congratulations, Valentyna. Be ready for your trip to America!" I felt very excited, was eager for new experiences, impressions and hard work as a JFDP exchange program fellow–a US State Department-funded program that identifies the most accomplished young faculty from Soviet successor countries (Armenia, Azerbaijan, Georgia, Kazakhstan, Kyrgyzstan, Moldova, Russia, Ukraine and others).

I was the recipient of one of ninety-two 11-month American Council, Washington, D.C. Scholarship Awards, August 2000–July 2001, from the Newly Independent States (NIS) of the former Soviet Union. The 2000–2001 academic years were especially remarkable for me and Chernivtsi National University (Ukraine): among 21 Ukrainian JFDP visiting scholars 3 were from my home institute. My colleagues were affiliated with the University of Tennessee–Knoxville, Michigan State University, and in my case–the University of Iowa.

I came to the USA from the Ukrainian city of Chernivtsi. Chernivtsi continues to hold a prominent position among other modern Ukrainian and Eastern European cities with its majestic image, unforgettable sights, and architectural places of interest. Its complex political history has led to a very mixed population (more than 240,600 people), including Russians, Moldavians, Poles, Romanians, Hungarians, and Jews. As a professor at Chernivtsi National University (CNU), I taught a variety of subjects such as EFL/ESL (English as a Foreign/Second Language), Linguistics, Lexicology, Methods in Teaching, and so forth. Since my graduation from the CNU, I have interest in Philology and Pedagogy. I contributed to various initiatives at the CNU while doing my research in TEFL/Applied Linguistics and coordinated international initiatives for regional institution building, curriculum expansion, and discussion of new pedagogy with colleagues from Ukraine, and abroad.

Professional and Cross–Cultural Experiences

I have never had the opportunity for such a lengthy stay in any country. Those eleven months during 2000–2001 have allowed me to live in the US and experience American life as an insider. During that time I was able enrich my linguistic skills and my knowledge of American culture. I also improved my vocabulary and perfected my knowledge of English. This helped me understand the intricate realities of the American society. This all brought to life for me the visual, aural and tactile scenes of daily life in America.

Thanks to constant contact with my coordinators and the staff at the Center for Russian, East European, and Eurasian Studies, as well as with my academic advisors, colleagues, and students of the Linguistic Department, I came to know how the American academic institute worked. We oftentimes compared experiences, teaching methodologies, personal or national/international approaches and trends. We've read current articles in our field and then discussed them in the light of the most current theories. The kind of knowledge and experiences we shared during face to face conversations could not be learned from books alone. That kind of inquisitive interactivity helped break down stereotypical ways of thinking and led to mutual understanding.

I took part in the work of the Linguistic Center (Center for Applied Linguistics) in Washington, D.C., and the International Women's Club in Iowa City. I gave an interview on radio about the impact of American Exchange Programs upon education in Ukrainian schools and universities.

I happily shared information about my country and home university with the students during my presentations: "Life in Post-Soviet Ukraine" in the course "Introduction to Russia, the Soviet Union and Its Successor States", and "National Psychological Features of Ukrainian National Character" presented during a Conversation Skill class. I became a USA TESOL member and presented at the 35th Annual International TESOL 2001 Convention "Gateway to the Future." In addition, I presented at CICLing-2001, the 2nd International Conference on Intelligent Text Processing and Computational Linguistics in Mexico City in February 2001.

After the 2000–2001 academic years were over, I served as an Intern in the Iowa Intensive English Program (IIEP). It allowed me to apply new knowledge of the academic field in a practical setting. I had a variety of experiences in working with international students enrolled in the IIEP, an academic English program designed to prepare students for study in a college or university in the United States. I taught the beginning-level students who needed extra assistance due to their low level of proficiency. Sometimes I worked with the students independently and sometimes in the classroom with the students' regular instructor. The areas that I taught included reading, writing, and grammar. In addition, I collaborated with IIEP program instructors, and participated in all student field trips to local areas of cultural interest.

I have benefited from my experience in working with students from all over the world who have come to the United States to learn English and pursue a post secondary education. I tried to work very hard this year and have grown enormously from the opportunity to live, study, and work in the United Sates. I definitely knew what to tell my students in Ukraine who were waiting for me and eager to share my US experience.

We Are Different

When a person comes to a country for the first time, his/her impressions are especially vivid. I found the uniqueness of Americans is that they inquire where you have come from, what your job is, how you like America and how long you are staying here. Unfortunately, the Americans don't know a lot about Ukraine. While introducing myself and my home country, I always was asked: "Ukraine? Where is it?" So, I explained that it's a sovereign state in Eastern Europe between Russia and Turkey. Ukraine is not a part of Russia! It's a small picturesque land with yellow wheat fields and pure blue sky (the Ukrainian national flag colors). It's a young country which celebrates only the 15th anniversary of its Independence in 2006. Americans, on the contrary, have celebrated 230 years of Independence this year!

We have much in common but yet we are different, with our own habits, customs and traditions. New Year celebrations (December 31st–January 1st) in Ukraine are more popular than in the U.S. Ukrainians celebrate Christmas on January 7th, while Americans celebrate it on December 25th. On September 1st we celebrate Day of Knowledge–the beginning of a new academic year in all the Ukrainian schools and colleges. In America the fall semester starts in different states not on the same day. The usual age of graduation of higher educational establishments in Ukraine is 21–23. In America it is 24–26. Our usual lunch time is from 1 until 2 pm or from 2 until 3 pm. In America it always starts at noon – 12 pm. The Americans like to talk about their families, traveling and sports. They do not like to talk about salaries, religion and politics. All these topics are discussed by my countrymen. Most Ukrainians live in apartments. In America mostly people live in houses. American fast food is not very popular in Ukraine. Americans clothes and footwear are simple and casual: pants, shorts/t-shirts and sneakers/flip-flops. Ukrainians wear stylish clothes and shoes.

The Americans like sociability. I think this feeling is reflected in the houses in the U.S. which have no hedges or fences separating them from the pavement or from each other. There are none of those little shut-off gardens, generally just a strip of grass with trees. With this sociability goes overwhelming hospitality. I don't think any door in the world is more open to the stranger than in an American home. You are taken to parties at the houses of your friends and your friends' friends. You are invited to theaters, dinners, sports meetings, and motor trips. From the first minute you are on "first name" terms with the people you meet. They all show the keenest interest in your affairs.

The Americans like new things. They love change, and call it "the spirit of adventure", a spirit that they think is more characteristic of America than of Europe. There may be something in this. There was a very interesting remark in a book by an English writer giving what he thought was a reason for this American characteristic. He wrote: "We in England, and the French, the Germans, the Italians, even the Russians, have all got one thing in common – we are descended from the men who stayed behind. In the USA they are descended from the folk who moved away." So in my eyes the Americans still like to "move away", to change homes and jobs. They seem to be constantly pulling down old and often quite beautiful houses or throwing away things merely because they are old.

Conclusion

After spending nearly a year in America, I had mixed feelings about returning home. It was so hard, confusing, and complicated to be in the U.S. I was happy on one side to leave because I wanted to see my family, friends, and colleagues in Ukraine. I was so excited to share with them my new ideas and what I learned in America. Conversely, it was difficult to part with my American friends, students from all over the world, and JFDP 2000–2001 fellows. I felt sad because I didn't know if we would be able to meet again. Many of them went off to colleges in different states and countries. I knew it would be hard to keep in contact. I hoped we would keep in touch, and some day we would reunite. I just wanted to be optimistic and believed in that. I dreamed that I could come back some day to the U.S. where people remembered me. It was hard to say goodbye, because it was a fantastic time. I didn't want to leave.

I am grateful for the support I had from my hospitable Ukrainian and American friends. They always helped me and understood when I was homesick. Their support was very important for me. I am really thankful to all my colleagues and teachers. I love and will always love the people who surrounded me.

Changing the Landscape

Oksana Maslovskaya

– Russia –

$\mathcal{M}$y alma mater, Eastern State Technical University (FESTU) is situated in Vladivostok city–edge point of Russian south-eastern border. In 1991, I graduated from FESTU with honors. Then I served as Assistant Professor (1991-1995) and Senior Teacher (1999-2003) at the Department of Architecture and Site Planning of the same university. My responsibilities included teaching architectural design studio, architectural composition, and drawing courses.

The first years of work as a qualified specialist were especially fruitful in architectural practice. This period I has designed more than thirty projects of cities centers, suburban settlements, administrative buildings, high-, middle- and low-rise housing. Some of the projects had win or placed in national and international design competitions. In 1999, I became a member of the Union of Architects of Russia. A big achievement of the year 2002 was gaining the grant on Junior Faculty Development Program for the study in US. I was placed at Landscape Architecture Program, Oklahoma State University, Stillwater (OSU), OK, as a Visiting Scholar for the 2002-2003 academic years.

First Impressions

Packing the baggage, flying on planes to Moscow and than to USA, I was thinking about immediate life perspectives and my life-span as a whole. I was full of resolve to make ongoing year the richest and happiest time in my life. The "AeroSmith" band was right when singing: "Anything you want you'll get it, anything you need you'll get it." As it is often happening, I was successful in fulfilling all kinds of my goals that period, even more than I could imagine.

However, despite my pretentious expectations, the first impressions were dull. Landscape of my host state Oklahoma for the main part has brownish-gray and yellowish-gray colors. The countable green spaces were obviously man-made. In the city of Stillwater, where University was situated, there weren't any natural water resource, only artificial Lake Boomer.

I was born in Vladivostok, which is in Primorye region – richest region on natural resources. I was used to admire by the beautiful combination of horizontal lines of the sea and dynamic skylines of forest covered hills. We have unusual neighborhood of tundra and tropic plants here, countless quantity of rivers, creeks, lakes and waterfalls. The city of Vladivostok is surrounded by the sea from the south, east and west. Hence, I was distressed by the flat nature environment in Oklahoma.

However, dryness of nature in Oklahoma was compensated, first of all, by warmth and hospitality of people living there. They always asked on question friendly and thoroughly, in some cases offering you to guide to desired place. They say, it's one of the Southerners qualities. It's intensified by small size of Stillwater. The climate of almost country size city allows communicating in humane way. The second compensation for nature dryness was gorgeous manmade landscapes: build works, students and professional projects. In the third place, my cheerful attitude ("this year must be the best") allowed me to focus rather on pluses than on minuses.

I had read in Oklahoma guidebook: "Imagine living life the way you've always dreamed…The time is now…The place is Oklahoma." In spite of difference in interpretations of readings this prediction was definitely about me. The year 2002-2003 have changed all my life. One accomplishment concerns my professional development and second one concerns even the biggest achievement: birth of my daughter Gallina. I always dream about happiness of maternity, and it was double miracle God give me the chance to become a mother that wonderful year.

University

At first the placement to the Landscape Architecture Program at OSU perplexed me. After several talking with my advisor Dr. Leider and other faculty members, I had realized the explanation of this. For the main part of my professional career I was interested in Urban Planning. This aspect belongs in US rather to Landscape Architecture than to Architecture itself. In US educational system and professional practice there were divided more than century ago.

The second confusing difference from Russia educational system was disposition of interior design, landscape architecture, architecture itself, visual arts department in different schools. I didn't want to loose any branch in this row. My mentor Dr. Nemechek decided this problem easily by inviting me to the year beginning faculty party. She acquainted me with almost all OSU professors. By virtue of this fact all following year I was able to communicate freely with many faculty members in any department interesting for me.

My selection in observing courses encompassed different kinds of Schools (Landscape Architecture, Architecture, Interior Design, and Educational Curriculum) and courses (historical, theoretical and practical) in order to observe the wider range of design programs in OSU. I was studying the philosophy, history, decision making, major concepts and terms in the curriculum development and structure attending the course *Curriculum Issues* in the School of Curriculum and Educational Leadership at the College of Education.

At the same time I was studying the historical and theoretical issues in architecture attending the course of Dr. Hunser *History and Theory of Early Modern Architecture* in the School of Architecture at the College of Engineering, Architecture and Technology. At the Department of Design, Housing and Merchandising in the College of Human Environmental Sciences I had choose the course *Environmental Perspectives on Apparel and Interior Design* that analyzes design, development and use of the built environment from physical, technological, economic, political, religious, social and aesthetic perspectives.

I had chosen several courses at Landscape Architecture Program in College of Agricultural Sciences and Natural Resources. There were *Land Use and Community Planning, Recreation Planning, Landscape Architectural Design IV and VI*. These courses met my objectives to study American system of Landscape Architecture and Site Planning. They embrace the theoretical and practical aspects, and also gave me the unique possibility to participate in the teaching process.

This period of my life was not only about education. This extraordinary year I had visiting a number of North American cities: Washington, Chicago, Minneapolis, Dallas, Oklahoma City, Tulsa, Bartlesville, Guthrie. Concerts, movies, museums, meeting with interesting people were also in my list. Local newspapers issues two articles about my advisor and me. In April my husband and I offered our North American colleagues and students the presentation about Far Eastern State Technical University and our School of Architecture as well as about ancient and contemporary Russian architecture and urban design.

As a main goal of Junior Faculty Development Program I was seeing the developing the *Urban Settlement Design and Planning* course outline. As every fellow of JFDP I was studying books and other materials on this subject, researching existing syllabi, observing courses in university, consulting with professors teaching in these areas in order to achieve this goal. However, the result was greater: all gathered materials built the grounds for opening entire landscape design education program in my home city Vladivostok.

Baby

The biggest result was, however, birth of Gallina. Dr. Leider was amaze I didn't come to his lecture that day. What was the surprise we are not family of two with my husband, but we are already family of three! I remain to be active all the time. Even in hospital where my husband and I spend only one and a half of days, we were meeting with our colleagues. The theme of talking was not professional issues, but newborn name, weight and height, caring problems, and other, to say you the truth.

The impression from Stillwater women's clinic and hospital was very good: polite and friendly personal, present-day level of equipment, accurate interiors. I'm very glad that my daughter was born in US, and I didn't counter numeral problems of contemporary Russian medical system. It's also very big accomplishment of US planning strategy that cities there have for the most part user-friendly environment. I understood that "What's good for people with disabilities can be good for everyone." Automatic doors, sloped doorways are very convenient for walking with stroller.

Despite these conveniences, at the end of first week I finally understood how I'm tired. As I had read from "Baby Talk" magazine one of the thing that is beyond a new mom's imagination is "Finishing your coffee while it's still hot". However another one unimaginable thing is "Feeling any happier than you do right now".

After spending almost a year in Stillwater, OK, I find myself loving Oklahoma. It wasn't because of only living there for ten months. And it wasn't even because Oklahoma became birthplace of my daughter. It is much deeper, it's part of me: Oklahoma experience gave me happiness of motherhood as well as inception to development of professional career. Living in foreign country and overcoming the challenges, I became more psychologically maturated as human.

Back to USA

Back to Russia I finally realize that my placement to the Landscape Architecture Department was not accident. The necessity of Landscape Design educational program in Vladivostok was clearly evident. There is the big contrast between beautiful nature and poor roads condition, neglected squares, abandoned parks. The contrast between nature environment and manmade landscape in Oklahoma has the same power but vise versa direction.

The idea to organize Landscape Design Department was approved by President of Vladivostok State University of Economy and Service (VSUES) Dr. Lazarev. Summer 2003 Landscape Design Department (LDD) at VSUES was established. My husband Dr. Ignatov came on Head of Department, and I became Associate Professor of LDD. There are seven faculty members in our department now. It's small, but very active and efficient one.

During 2003-2006 colleagues and I have developed two textbooks, different course programs, and design programs for all years of study. Almost every faculty member uses the Power Point Program, works with Multimedia, publishes course materials in Internet, and encourages students to review most interesting Internet sites. Landscape Design Department as a part of VSUES Web site is regularly updated: we are adding educational materials and presenting information about our activities. In 2005 our department has organized the long-distance National Design Competition of Diploma Projects with 9 universities and 32 projects participated in it.

My professional career was also turned into landscape design. As a member of team or only author I had designed about 15 projects of parks, city squares and residential landscape designs. The guidance in student's projects is nevertheless bigger part of my work now. As a part of community service we developed landscape design projects for Primorye Veterans Hospital, several schools and colleges, VSUES campus. We are collaborating with American partner developing ideas of big-scale "Canem World" park in California. In realization of non-profit and commercial projects we collaborate with professional landscape design studios and Vladivostok Botanical Garden.

In the past 3 years our students have won or placed 12 times in national and regional design competition. Our most outstanding successes include: 3 diplomas for the 2005 National Architecture and Design Competition of Diploma Projects; Gold Medal for the 2005 International Design Competition "DV-Zodchestvo." Landscape of Vladivostok is changing. Thank Junior Faculty Development Program; it wouldn't be done without help of them.

Notes about Arts and Culture in America

Yelena Kondaurova, PhD

– Kazakhstan –

Having been a musicologist and teacher of some musical theoretical disciplines at the Kazakh National Conservatory in Almaty, Kazakhstan since 1988, I was honored to be a Junior Faculty Development Program fellow in Arts Management field for 2004-2005 academic year. So, I was placed at the Indiana University, Bloomington in order to develop Arts Management course through attending and observing different classes, learning teaching methodology of Arts Administration Program at IU School of Public and Environmental Affairs.

It seemed I was lucky with my placement on different reasons. The first, Bloomington was situated almost at the same geographical latitude, like my hometown was; that was why I had no any problems with climate adaptation and felt comfortable there. The second, eight of the JFDP fellows were also placed at IU, and two my roommates came with me from the same region, Central Eurasia, Kazakhstan and Kyrgyzstan. Besides, I met a lot of my countrymen in Bloomington; moreover, many faculties and students spoke Russian at our host Department, IU Uralic and Inner Asian Studies Center. The listed things facilitated my "entrance" in new environment, helped to overcome my homesick and make my stay in Bloomington very pleasant and productive.

Finally, in despite on the town was comparatively small, there were a great number of institutions for arts and culture, which Bloomington was famous for. According to information from the IU web-site, this town was named "Mecca for Arts and Culture" and it was the best thing for me! Due to my academic category, to learn about arts and culture in the USA was an important part of my program. Therefore I got a good opportunity to attend various arts and cultural events for this period, in which I was very interested either as an arts manager, arts critic, musicologist, and just enjoyed them as a friend of arts and culture. In the whole, I undertook museum and theater tours in order to become acquainted with their working process, visited different exhibitions, art fairs, performances, festivals, concerts, lectures and colloquiums from the IU School of Music. Fortunately, many buildings and halls, where cultural events usually took place, were located on the IU campus area; there were IU Art Museum, William Hammond Mathers Museum of World Cultures, Wylie House Museum, Marshall Black Culture Center, IU Auditorium, Lee Norvelle Theater and Drama Center, the Musical Arts Center, Auer Concert Hall, Ford-Crawford Hall, the Recital Hall, etc. along them. Other ones were set out downtown, ten minutes walking from the University; there were the Buskirk-Chumley Theater, the Wonder Lab Museum of Science, Health & Technology, the Monroe County History Center, John Waldron Arts Center, many Galleries and Cinema. Since I lived nearby the campus, I was attending cultural events almost daily.

Of course, I was very impressed of everything concerning arts and cultural life in Bloomington. Later, when I was traveling about America during breaks and holidays, I understood that well-developed cultural sphere has been typical for this country, and Bloomington was not an exception. At that time I was trying to answer key questions to clarify for myself phenomena of arts and culture in the US:

What were the arts and culture for Americans? Which elements were the most important in their definitions?

What were secrets and reasons of great success and popularity for arts productions and events in the US?

I also had so many "why" regarding arts and culture issues.

The first step on the way to my understanding of these things suddenly had been done at one of my ESL classes with a private tutor, when he offered me to discuss the topic "Arts and Culture". The following passage from our dialogue became crucial for me:

How do you think, what is culture? He asked.

Culture is everything around us. I replied.

What about cars and buildings? Are they too?

They are also products of culture. However, when you have asked me to define culture, you probably meant only arts as a part of culture. Definitions of arts and culture are often mixing up.

For me, an essence of the above mentioned conversation became a point about limits, connections and interactions between culture, arts and social life. Most of people could perceive arts in social and cultural context; on the other hand, usually they rarely separated each element in their mind for themselves. Was it a permanent error or normality? I made sure, that it was a natural regularity. Besides, in the US arts, culture and social life were very close to each other, and this peculiarity was one of reasons, why cultural production was so called for there.

To prove their interdependence, I just refer to typical for this country kind of activity, as volunteer work for cultural and social organizations and events is. My fellows and I participated ourselves as volunteers in some activities organized by our host department, Uralic and Inner Asian Studies Center. We presented Russian/Cyrillic alphabet and some Russian/Kazakh/Kyrgyz/Tajik words, phrases writing and pronunciation at Bloomington Multicultural Festival in September and Lotus Blossom Festival in March; we taught, how to make with pieces of paper the simplest models of the nomadic house, "yurt", and told folk Kazakh, Kyrgyz, Tajik and Uzbek stories, tales and legends for children of Bloomington at Children's Navrus. During Navrus celebration at IU we cooked national food, and were singing, dancing, playing national music. My fellows and I also gave several live presentations about culture of Central Eurasia countries, sang national and Russian songs at concerts for retired communities of Bloomington. At the end of the JFDP program each of us got five or six Certificates of Appreciation with Thank You Letters from Indiana University for our volunteer work!

At the same time, I could see that a lot of other people attended meetings and events, participated in activities of various communities; they also had been involved in the same process, where arts, cultural and social parts functioned in equal measure. Their combination was the main reason, why each person could find somewhat interesting and useful for self-realization or just for fun. On the other hand, people's involvement in implementation of cultural projects was giving additional impulses for creativity and furthering of "an extra interest" towards culture and arts. All these things additionally attracted people to cultural sphere and enhanced its popularity either for its friends and professionals! Having primarily been along volunteers, non-professional participants or parts of audience at social cultural events, many of them became then frequenters of concert halls, theatres, museums, etc.

Another reason of popularity for arts and culture in America I would define as cultural diversity and pluralism, multiculturalism and multi-stylistics. I think, their roots are based on the phenomenon of "melting pot", where everything and everyone may have a place or find it. Every time I was wondering with great quantity of different Diasporas, living in their districts such as Chinatown, Ukrainian Village or "Little Italy", Russian and International Markets, restaurants with many kinds of special cuisines and numbers of cultural Latino, Tibetan, Mongolian, Chinese, Korean, Azeri, Indonesian, etc. festivals.

Regarding professional arts, I was astounded for the first time, when I had found out the original of "Atelier" by Pablo Picasso at IU Art Museum in Bloomington; I couldn't imagine the same thing in my home country. Later I couldn't express all my feelings, when I was walking downtown Chicago and looking at Picasso's sculpture of "Woman-Bird", which had been built right on the Daley Center Plaza! I also was very exited and impressed with works of impressionists, pointillists and futurists, which were gathered at Art Institute of Chicago. I thought: this collection of them was the best one! I was surprised as well, when I made sure, that numbers of pictures by Marc Shagal were much more there than at exposition of Russian Museum, Saint-Petersburg, Russia.

Having attended concerts and performances wherever and whenever it was possible, I made sure as well, that works of Russian composers were popular too and playing very often, and Igor Stravinsky's "Star" was there on the Hollywood Boulevard, Los Angeles, CA. Of course, a lot of musical works of other different composers from all styles, directions and nationalities were playing and performing everywhere at concert halls, theatres, hard rock and jazz café, outdoors' performances during festivals, holidays and week-ends. Even in so small town, like Bloomington was, I enjoyed live music every day at IU Musical Art Center and many other music halls. Besides, there were so many musical outdoor events right on Bloomington's streets, squares, parks and lawns in a time of Fourth Street Festival of the Arts in Labor Day week-end, Lotus Music World & Arts Festival in fall, Early Music Festival in May, Summer Music Festival, The Fourth of July parade and firework, just in worm week-ends.

I learned "top secrets" of success for arts and culture in America, when I had taken an internship at Office of Marketing & Publicity, IU School of Music. Having participated in its working projects as an administrative assistant, I got an opportunity to compare my new empirical knowledge with practical experience.

Honestly, at the beginning of my internship I was a little bit disappointed, because it seemed to me, that my supervisor was asking me to do only the easiest and unimportant job. I was unable to accept as serious tasks, for example, his requests to check and put in alphabetical order all files of IU School of Music faculties, or scan their photos to update and complete a series of profiles on IU website. However, after I had finished one of projects with inventory and systemizing of all IU School of Music posters since 1987, when I composed and submit their catalogue, he thanked me, and I appreciated his intention to help me to clarify many things through my own practice. In the hole, on example of the office, I understood, that:

- There were not unimportant details in organization and administration for arts and culture in the US; everything was important as an element or part of one general process,
- For successful protection, promotion the cultural sector, keeping its positive image, business for arts and culture always took attention, serious attitude, time, well-planned and prepared job of many people, as any other business did.

These peculiarities and characteristics are functioning in America indeed everywhere in everything. That is why arts and culture have so high level status there.

I express my sincere delight of arts and culture in the USA; now I know that my enhanced cultural experience influenced me in a positive way. Living again in my home country, Kazakhstan, I believe, that my enriched cultural knowledge will be resourceful and helpful for my activities on behalf of the local community.

Nine Months that Proved to be Ten Years' Inspiration

Maryna Babenko, PhD

– Ukraine –

A graduate from one of the oldest Ukrainian Universities, Vasyl Karazin National University (Kharkiv), I had had more than ten years of practical experience as an EFL teacher trainer before I went to the USA on the exchange program. Like everyone who wants to master their knowledge of the subject they teach, I was eager "to sponge" every piece of information concerning English-speaking communities all over the world. I've always considered it very important to know as much as possible about the country and the people whose language I teach. By the time I went to the USA, I had read many books on American studies and had quite a lot of experience in communication with American teachers who had visited Ukraine on exchange programs. Professor Jack Pickering and his wife Susan were among them. They were very supportive and patient to answer all our questions concerning the USA, its education system, history, people, and cultural diversity. Dr. Pickering taught American Literature. In addition to that he observed some classes we taught and gave his feedback.

When I was told about the new program that was administered in Ukraine for the first time, I did not hesitate a moment. That was the Junior Faculty Development Program. I prepared the statement of purpose and filled out the application.

It is quite natural for people to have hobbies, mine was collecting limericks, and from time to time I even tried to create my own ones. Therefore, I began my statement of purpose with the following rhyme:

There was a teacher trainer Maryna
Who taught English in her native Ukraina [ukra'i:na].
She filled out the application
for Education Administration.
Guess what answer got Maryna?

And the answer was "yes!". This is how my life as a part of Missouri University community started on August 13, 1996 in a small American town Columbia.

I often recollect the words by James Mincher, a U.S. novelist, *"If you reject the food, ignore the customs, fear the religion, and avoid people, you might [as well] stay home. You are like a pebble thrown into water: you become wet on the surface, but you are never part of the water".* I was eager to become "part of the water", that is why I met people, talked to them, asked question, participated in every activity. The events and encounters were so numerous that a mere enumeration of them would take much space.

The JFDP Program is very flexible, it allows the participants not only to conduct scientific research, but also attend classes, visit scientific conferences, use the library resources. In addition to that every participant came to be involved in "socializing" and routine activities, such as visiting banks, getting an ATM card, obtaining money from the ATM-machine, even talking to a plumber! All those required some skills and often cultural background knowledge.

The most important thing was that only after I became a part of the multi-national community of the University did I fully recognize that I am a representative of the independent state, Ukraine, on the American land. My mentor, Ms. Irene Juzkiw, ELSP Program director at MU, was a Ukrainian American. She was born in the USA, but her parents moved to America from Ukraine in the 1940s. I always felt her heart was still with her roots, in Ukraine...

International students and visiting scholars on campus were involved into various activities, for example, the International Bazaar, where all communities presented some information about their countries, demonstrated national clothes, and cooked national dishes. At this bazaar, we had a joint booth for representatives from the former Soviet Union countries. Among them there were people from Ukraine, Russia, Kazakhstan, Belarus, Latvia, and Estonia. There was a long line in front of our booth when we treated everybody with our "pelmeny" and "vareniki"!

On campus there were two independent non-profit organizations for international students: "International Friends" and "Friends of Internationals". I was eagerly involved into all the activities of these groups. They arranged dinners, shopping, tours for international students. With the help of these organizations I spent two wonderful weeks in Arkansas ("International Christmas"), and Thanksgiving-1997 in a little town Montgomery-City, MO. My friend Dr. Nina Shekhovtsova (a JFDP fellow from Russia) and I were invited to elementary schools in Columbia and Montgomery to tell American children about our countries. Though the kids knew very little about Russia – "it was in their computers", as they told us-the name "Ukraine" did not ring the bell at all! Hopefully, they knew a little more about Ukraine after our meeting.

Career was always very important for me, and I had always had to choose between my family and my career. My son was six when I went to the USA for this exchange program, and, believe me, it was not a very easy decision to part with him for almost a year! When I came back to Kharkiv, he told me that if he had known I would be away for so long he would have never let me go... Was my career at that time interfering with my family life? Now I understand that the answer is negative, because the knowledge and experience I gained from participation in the JFDP turned out to be invaluable for me.

To develop professionally I attended various classes at the University of Missouri-Columbia. I took four classes in the fall semester, and it was fun to become a student again after so many years of teaching! Also, it was quite a difficult task to get ready for all those classes. Only after I became a student again did I realize how hard American students had to work to earn the necessary credits. In the spring term I took only two classes in order to concentrate on the Methods of ESL/EFL teaching and Writing. In addition to that, I spent many hours in the library reading books and journals and trying to find material for my philological research.

It was very useful for me as a professional teacher trainer to get acquainted with the American system of teaching and training. My mentor and I attended three professional conferences. The one in Orlando, FL, was the best and most memorable. That was the TESOL Convention, the most important annual event for teachers of English as a second/foreign language all over the world. The next year, after I came back to Ukraine, I participated in the contest and was awarded a TESL/TEFL Travel Grant to attend another annual convention, this time in Seattle, WA. It was also very interesting and informative, but the one in Orlando was the first, therefore, more memorable. Or might it be because of the fantastic and fascinating world of Disney, Universal Studios, and the Sea World almost next door? In Orlando there was a real reunion of the JFDP Fellows from Ukraine: there were eight of us, coming from different states of the USA and exchanging our impressions about our stay in the country. Unfortunately, that year the Program experienced some financial difficulties and the joint JFDP Conference in Iowa was cancelled; therefore, twenty JFDP Ukrainians could communicate only via e-mail. You can imagine how important that evening in Orlando was! Another memorable event in Orlando was the meeting with the representatives of TESOL-Ukraine who came to the Convention as guests of TESOL. This trip from Ukraine was organized with the help of another Ukrainian American, a wonderful woman Zirka Voronka.

Celebrating holidays in Columbia is another page. International Women's Day is not widely celebrated in the United States, but the University International Center organized a panel discussion on that day. Eight women (including me) from various countries were invited to speak about their countries, the status of women in their societies. That was a difficult task and a great honor to represent Ukrainian women. I was doing my best to prepare for that discussion, trying to use Internet facilities to find out some fresh information about the current situation in Ukraine. One cannot imagine how much time I spent, as the most numerous sites were those where Ukrainian women wanted to find husbands abroad or foreign men sought for Ukrainian girls! Yes, I am absolutely positive that our women are the most wonderful, but ten years ago there were much more problems that Ukrainian women were concerned of: unemployment, underpayment, and many others.

Another flashback is connected with Philadelphia. That was my dream to visit this city, because it is the real heart of America, the place of birth of the USA. I was planning the trip beforehand. Using Internet I found a lot of information about the location of various historical sights in the city. I read so much about the Independence Hall, the Betsy Ross House that I could imagine every place, every room... In Philadelphia I had some "cultural experience" visiting a Women's Gardening Club. To tell the truth, I felt being Eliza Doolittle at this meeting with all those formal closing (no trousers!) and polite "How do you do?' instead of Missourian "Hi!". Oh yes, in December 1996 in Philadelphia I felt more like a real "showme-ress"...

While experiencing another culture and meeting various people, I began to understand my own culture and my own people better. *"Own only what you can carry with you: know language, know countries, know people. Let your memory be your travel bag"* (Alexander Solzhenitsin, Russian novelist).

Ten years ago that letter with "congratulations!" opened a vivid and fruitful page in my life. I am so deeply grateful to those wonderful people I met in the USA, and also to those who arranged and financed this exchange visit. To my belief, participating in the JFDP opened new horizons in front of me, taught how to develop my abilities and realize my potential. The Program was like a jump-off ground for all my life and career.

A Few Miniature Deliberations on the Program in Retrospect

Rakhiya Bekbayeva

– Kazakhstan –

Half way on the plane from Almaty, Kazakhstan, to the country of the final destination, the United States, I could not help thinking about the family I was leaving behind: a husband and three children. How would they live for almost a year without me, a major breadwinner and caretaker in the family? Would my children feel secure or would they have to go through many challenges without their mom? I promised I would get my younger son, Tleules (13 years old) and my daughter Raushan (11) to the US in three months as the program allowed. My eldest son, a more self-reliant and independent person, was a student at one of the universities at that time. Having left my kids with their father, unemployed and, in fact, having little will to change his life, I was all but feeling righteous about the decisions I had made.

Behind was a full-time teaching job at the University of World Languages in Almaty, as well as jobs in three more institutions totaling to more than 50 hours of instruction only. Popularity of the English language let me and hundreds of other Kazakhstani English language teachers fill in the niche and provided opportunity to earn for a living. However, as the interest to the English language was increasing steadily, so were the requirements for its instruction, which in turn opened new avenues for self-study and professional development?

Partly to cater mounting requirements and being to a certain extent discontented by the compensation I had been receiving for overwork, I applied to the Junior Faculty Development Program. Acquiring new techniques in a foreign language teaching, developing a program on Business Communication and getting updated resources were all I needed to change my existing career patterns and professional growth. Hardly did I expect that eleven months in the United States on the program would be a U-turn not only for my future career, but also for my family and my personal life.

Impact of People

With hindsight, I can say that people I met in the US brought about the most remarkable influence. KU professors who lent me furniture and other staff for the apartment; an elderly couple who gave me directions and even paid for a taxi when I arrived at the wrong hotel in Scottsdale, Arizona; a couple who gave me frequent rides to the grocery store to stock food for a week – these are just a few examples of generosity and kindness for which I feel overwhelmingly grateful to the American people.

Initial contacts at the University of Kansas (KU), my host university, were the people from the International Programs Office who helped me find an apartment, select courses, and showed around the city. Professors from the Department of Communication Studies at KU helped me to adjust to the new environment and lent me their hands. Be it settling at the new place or seeking for professional advice, everyone was there for me willing to share anything. My mentors on the program, Diana Carlin and Paul Friedman, became role models of skillfulness and kindheartedness. It is still a mystery to me how Diana, who in addition to her teaching worked as an Assistant Provost Marshall and was involved in various research projects and textbook writing, found time and energy not only to advise me professionally, but also to show different aspects of life in the United States. My kids and I gained unforgettable experience of Christmas holidays with Diana's family and friends and the kids stayed in her place while I was at the conference in Washington DC.

I agreed to continue teaching the course on the cross-cultural communication started by a previous-year JFDP scholar from Russia even before I arrived at KU, during the orientation week in Delaware. The Russian scholar who had talked me into accepting the offer was very persuasive. I also believed that teaching the course would speed up the adaptation process by providing more time for work and less time for anxiety. Besides, work waiting for me could not be more challenging than work I used to have in my home country.

Nevertheless, on the first day of classes, I barely had enough courage to enter the room and face the students. Well, I did have more than a decade of teaching behind me, but I had never taught American students, not to mention that I had little experience of communicating with native speakers. Had not it been for Paul, I would have felt intimidated and out of place.

Always prepared to lend a hand if needed, Paul made teaching of the course valuable and never-to-be-forgotten experience for me as a professional. Thanks to his support and positive attitude in dealing with daily challenges, I started feeling more and more confident in the classroom. Once he saw I established rapport with the students, he let me continue the course on my own.

Friends

Somehow, before my trip to the US I had an instilled perception that American people are not able to commit to long-term friendly relationships and cannot be considered real friends as we, in my culture, understand it. This stereotype, as well many others, did not stand a reality check and was soon toppled. Consequently, I had to reconsider the whole concept of friendship.

Having my younger children with me enriched both my life and that of the kids. They got their chance to see the world and obtained invaluable experience from attending a junior high school there. For me, it was a chance to meet more people outside the university setting and have first-hand knowledge of a school life in the US. Very shortly after their arrival, my kids who spoke conversational English were happily intermingling with other American teens at school. Their English language teacher, Kim Kreicker, devoted enormous amount of time to the kids in her ESL class showing them as much of the American life as possible.

Now I cannot even recall when Kim became a key figure in the life of my kids. When she found out about our enormous eagerness to see more of the country, which did not correspond to the limited resources we had, Kim came up with different suggestions for cheap and easy travel. She ended up offering to take us to the Disneyworld in Florida, where she was planning to attend a conference. It was the first trip ever for which I did not have to arrange anything as Kim had taken care of everything: accommodation, transport, planning, and entertainment. I wrote on the wall calendar across the departure date, "Are we going to Florida?" as I could not believe that it was in fact happening. During more than a week trip with Kim, we found out more about the country, people, nature, life, and culture than from any other source of information.

When we returned to Kazakhstan, it was almost daily exchange of e-mails with our American friends that kept me from being smashed by harsh reality and a reverse cultural shock. In fact, even none of my relatives would do what my American friends have done for my family and me. Invaluable support received from my friends, Kim and her friend, Arla, helped me survive the toughest days and go through the painful divorce process a year after my return home. Their infinite enthusiasm and generosity brought my younger son, Tleules, to study his first year at the University of Kansas. That he would be able to return as an undergraduate student three years after we left the US was beyond my wildest dreams.

I feel blessed that I met so many wonderful people in the United States and many of them have become my closest friends. I realize that it might sound somewhat trite; however, I also understand how little genuine feeling these words are able to convey.

Culture

Staying in another country one becomes acutely aware of the differences between his own culture and that of the host country. Sometimes the difference might be negligible and most likely go undetected at home or while communicating with your country fellows. In a completely foreign environment, among people who share commonalities, you realize that this is not accepted in your culture. All of a sudden, you are inhibited by the norms of behavior or values of which you had never been aware.

It took time before I got used to replying optimistically with an anticipated "Fine, thank you" to perfunctory "How are you?" especially when I did not in fact feel fine. Moreover, doing it repeatedly, every time you see someone, struck me as something superfluous. I remember feeling extremely irritated at one point, when I was sitting in the office and overheard people in the university hall cheerfully exchanging insincere, in my view, greetings. It seemed to me that those people did not, indeed, care how another person felt and were just displaying extremely sugarcoated courtesy. Of course, the fact that at that very moment I was feeling desperately worried about my family added to the faulty perception.

It took time before I got used to not accepting some enthusiastic statements by the Americans literally. If somebody says, "I enjoyed talking to you. Let's go out someplace before you leave", it is not an explicit suggestion but just another expression of politeness and good will. It took time before I got used to shaking hands with men while being introduced or staying seated while a man or an elderly person is standing at your presence.

I found it strange that the elderly people live alone while some of their children live in the same city but in a different house. In my country, where several generations of the family live in one house, it would be something extraordinary as we are taught to revere the elderly and take care of them. The need to be self-reliant in order not to overburden children still seems alien to me. What is wrong if children take care of their elderly parents and, thus, pay off a small portion of care and love they had received? However, my experience in the US also taught me it is important to be tolerant and try to understand and accept the norms and traditions of another culture, no matter how unacceptable they might appear to you.

Identity

Perhaps any person in a foreign country feels as a kind of envoy representing the best his/her country has. The most challenging part in this case is imminent realization that many people you meet in the US, do not know what country you come from. Every time that happened, I had to do my best to help distinguish my country out of many "stans" on the world map. "Oh, you are from Pakistan?" "No, Kazakhstan is in Central Asia and it has ninth largest territory in the world". Mentioning the mightiest neighbors, Russia and China, helped a lot when there was no map at hand. Therefore, I was always pleasantly surprised when in the most unexpected settings outside academia I met people who not only knew where my country was located, but also had some intimate knowledge about it.

Having cleared the question of the home country, people would very often ask a question that usually caught me on the hop, "Is Kazakhstan a democratic state?" Discussing the issue of democracy and democratic values related to my home country had always been more a matter of subtle diplomacy than of straightforward truth. One can feel torn between the urge to report everything accurately and the necessity to stand for your home country and discuss the challenges it is facing in its development. I am afraid many people with whom I discussed those issues were left astounded by the lack of clear-cut answers.

Before arrival to the US, I had hardly contemplated on how heavy baggage of 18 years of marriage to a man from a very conventional family influenced my viewpoint. Interacting with the American people in different locations: students and professors in the academic setting, friends, and acquaintances during informal events, I was compelled to review everything, from the real meaning of my career to mere foundations of my family life and relationships with my husband and kids. As a result, I chose not to be passively carried away by seemingly lethargic and trouble-free current any longer, but instead redefine the essentials and reshape my life and career accordingly. I would like to think I emerged as a stronger and more determined character than I was before my American experience.

Academic Activities

The semester reports I found while drafting this essay took me back to the University of Kansas and all the activities I was involved in during the program. I wanted to accomplish many different things during the program: to gain knowledge of teaching techniques in the US universities, develop a new course of Business English to teach back in my home country, to expand information base in my field of study, to name a few. I ended up auditing courses on Effective Business Communication, Persuasive Speaking, Cross Cultural Negotiations, EFL Teaching Methods, Gender Communication, Business Writing, Organizational Behavior, Business Communication Projects, and Introduction to International Business offered by different departments and schools at KU. In addition to these, I avidly attended all possible computer courses (free for visiting scholars), seminars held by the Center for Teaching Excellency, and workshops offered by the Applied English Center. I attended National Communication Association annual convention in Chicago and presented a paper at the Thunderbird-EMU conference in Scottsdale, Arizona, and at the Mid TESOL and NAME (National Association for Multicultural Education) conference in Omaha, Nebraska.

When the program was over, I asked myself whether I managed to accomplish all the objectives I set initially. The positive answer, which was not that obvious then, is easier to articulate today. Today, everything I learnt in the US can be reviewed through the prism of the daily work and on-going process of professional development. Today, I can say that all those university courses that I audited, professors I met, and various activities that I was involved gave a powerful impetus to my career as an educator inspiring me to achieve more and learn more.

American National Character

Alissa Tolstokorova, PhD

– Ukraine –

After finishing my post-graduate studies and obtaining a PhD degree in Humanities in 1991, I was teaching in a small Southern city of Ukraine. The course American Studies which I taught at the Kherson State Pedagogical University incorporated such sections as history, political and administrative system, cultural heritage, urban life in the USA. The paradox of my situation as a lecture was that I was an "expert" in American Studies only theoretically, because I had to teach my students about the country which I have never visited myself and like my students knew of it only through books, periodicals, TV and occasional interactions with American visitors to Ukraine. It goes without saying that the most objective, detailed and reliable information about life in a country one can get only thought the first-hand experience in the country itself. This explains my long-cherished dream to visit "the land of opportunities", whose history and culture I was researching and teaching for many years. In 1999 I had a lucky chance to put my dream to practice by securing a fellowship for Junior Faculty Development program. Thanks to it I had an exciting year in the USA to work as a Visiting Scholar on curricula development in American Studies.

My program at the GMU Department of History and Art History of George Mason University, located in close proximity to the US capital–Washington DC, a centre of cultural, academic and political life, gave me an excellent opportunity to extend my knowledge not only in the field of American History, but in many aspects of social life in the USA. A possibility to have tours over the headquarters of the US administrative system - American Congress and White House, Department of State, Pentagon and FBI - gave me an insight into the foundations of US social system and a better understanding of factors, which shape the American mentality and national character.

Besides, my active membership in the GMU Art History Club allowed me to have a better idea about history and ethnic diversity in American multicultural community. This became possible thanks to the GMU Arts Bus study tours to exhibitions in National Gallery, Museum of Women's History and Smithsonian Institutions in Washington D.C., Museum of Modern Art, and Metropolitan Museum of Art, art exhibitions in Chelsea and Soho in New York City, Pennsylvania Museum of Modern Art and Archaeological Museum in Philadelphia. A history bus tour to historical places of Maryland Campaign by General Robert Lee, organized for students of the Department of History, was a substantial contribution not only to my historic awareness and knowledge of the Civil War events and its outstanding actors, but to my understanding of the Southern history and mentality in general.

A possibility of academic conferences attendance, provided by the JFDP administration, was also very helpful in terms of professional knowledge acquisition. The conference in American Culture and Popular Culture in New Orleans (April, 2000) gave a clear vision of newest trends and tendencies in Youth culture and in modern Arts, influence of European art on American architecture and music. A Feminist Expo Conference in Baltimore (March-April, 2000) was a good opportunity to enrich my professional knowledge of the US women's movement and its history, feminist agenda, women's issues in human rights and social security reform etc. it also allowed to develop professional linkages both with individual women activists and researchers, and with prominent American and international women's organizations and institutions.

A "human face" of American Individualism

My visit to the US was the first experience of a foreign culture in my life, And although from lectures at orientation sessions first at the Fulbright office in Kiev and later at Delaware University in Newark I was already warned about possible problems of the adaptation period in a foreign country and about a possibility to experience cultural shock during my first months in America, and despite I was forearmed with some basic knowledge of intercultural literacy, I still had to confront lots of cultural challenges both in my academic surrounding and in general day-to-day situations.

First of all, I discovered with surprise that despite my personal and professional interest in the "phenomenon of American civilization" and years of teaching American Studies to University students, my understanding of American cultural patters was, to put it mildly, somewhat abstract and far from real life. I guess the explanation to it is partly in the impact of American mass-media and video-industry. Because the patriotic intention of the "fourth branch of power" to bring to the world an exaggeratedly positive image of America as a powerful, prosperous society of equal opportunities is quite natural and understandable. This generalized image of the country as a "land of opportunities" is largely counted both on an average American and on the international community. But the problem is that it is often forgotten that one and the same means, which work well on the national ground, outside of American cultural context may turn into their opposite–a clearly negative image of the country, congested by individualism and consumerism, where the power of force and violence dominate traditional human values. The same works for other countries too. For example, over the years of the cold war a little smiling teddy bear, a charming symbol of the Moscow Olympic Games -1980, was considered by the soviet people to be a personification of their good will, open-heartedness and sociability. At the same time from the other side of the border this innocent toy was perceived as a hint on the fierce and unpredictable character of the notorious "Russian bear", or in other words--a potential trouble. I think that such a difference in perceptions and semantic implications of the same concepts depends on divergences in semantic basis and value rates in different cultures.

By analogy, the image of America as a superpower has patriotic connotations for those who perceive it form inside the country, but from oversees it is often associated with the image of the "world cop," ready to attack everyone who does not share traditional American values. Movies and serials about all-mighty American cops-the-supermen, who in any circumstances win the battle for justice and human dignity, for average Americans may symbolize a power of the law in their country and imply the inevitability of punishment for those who disobey it. At the same time, for international consumers of the American video-products, who observe the scenes of American virtual life from the criminal context of their own country, these "typically American" implications of the movies are irrelevant and meaningless. Really, can the "Texas Rangers" or the "Los Angeles Police" be of any help to a victim of burglars somewhere in Kiev, Moscow or Tokyo? Of course not! But then, what's the use of heroism and professional skills of American cops to a movie spectator in Ukraine, Belarus or the Ivory Coast? No use, no sense. However, the after-effect of these movies is very strong, because what they leave in the memory is a variety of bright images of insidious villains, an impression of America as a country of anarchy, criminality, and a world congested by individualism, where the power of force subdues traditional human values.

Luckily, the devil appeared to be not as black as it was painted by the American video-art. I did experience culture shock of which I was forewarned, but it was caused not by terrors of life in the country "of yellow devil," but by reality which in practice surpassed even my most optimistic expectations. The Americans, at least most of those with whom I had a chance to get in touch, did not fit the wide-spread image of pragmatic bourgeois-Yankees, whose only sense of life is work, money and profit. On the contrary, they turned to be sociable, supportive, dignified and spirited people with wide range of interests. This was a puzzle for me and a question I was much pondering on: "Why did American people seem so different face to face and when watched from oversees? Why do typical American screen characters--an aggressive "guy with the gun" and an invincible "superwoman"–$in real life turn to be so nice, attractive, slightly sentimental and even naïve?

I came to a conclusion that this happened because of profound intercultural differences in the perceptions and interpretations of basic qualities traditionally ascribed to the generic image of a "standard American" in the country itself and in the part of the world I come from. The discrepancy refers primarily to the concept of "individualism" often cited in mass-media, books, guides, commercials and movies, advertising American life-style, as a curb-stone to understanding the American national character. During our group's cultural orientation sessions first in Kiev Fulbright office and then at Delaware University it was also emphasized that recognition of individualism as a basic quality of the American mentality would facilitate adjustment to the new cultural setting for an international student.

It appeared, however, that semantic implications of this notion in the linguistic consciousness of Ukrainians and Americans are very different, if not opposite. Ukrainians (and probably all post-soviets) regard this concept as a clearly negative, congruent to selfishness and egocentrism, as a quality pertaining to those who live exclusively for themselves, often for the expense of others, disregarding their needs, interests and priorities. Individualism as a human quality is considered a sign of low spiritual development and is condemn and discouraged in Ukrainian cultural tradition. Contrary to it, in American mentality, as far as I understand it, individualism is associated with self-sufficiency and with ability "to take care of oneself", a social skill indispensable for survival in such a dynamic and competitive society as America. It is perceived as a capability to solve one's personal problems by one's own efforts, rather than by shifting the responsibility for their solution on the shoulders of one's significant others: friends, family, community.

In this sense individualism is welcome, encouraged and even cultivated in American society as a marker of social maturity of its citizens.

I want to share my reflections on the problem of divergences in linguistic consciousness in different cultures with my colleagues, aiming to attract attention to the dramatic impact of language stereotypes on the issues very distant from the philological domain. What I mean is that seemingly insignificant discrepancies in the semantic perceptions of similar concepts in different language systems may cause profound communication gaps, disruptions and result in misinterpretations of cultural standards, attitudinal conflicts and even hostility. That's why I want to highlight the importance of cross-cultural awareness and literacy in the system of humanitarian knowledge and especially in the area of international contacts for the sake of achieving mutual understanding and successful cooperation between nations.

American Mind As I See It

During my program at the GMU Department of History and Art History I had an opportunity to audit a course titled "American Minds" which was focused on the discussion of the situation of different social groups within the American cultural system and on problems of national identity. The professor who was teaching the class, a historian Dr. Jeffrey Stuart, soon became my good friend, because my presence in the class was welcome and encouraged as everyone wanted to know how the "American mind" is perceived by an outsider to the American culture, especially by a former soviet. During the classes I tried to answer all the questions of the professor and my fellow colleagues, although I must admit that it was somewhat difficult to be both honest and sincere in your evaluation of another country and at the same tactful and objective.

When the course was over the professor asked me if I want to write an essay to share my impressions and understanding of the main points of the course. I decided not to write the essay because I was afraid of my thoughts might lead me to some misunderstandings, and even hurt my dear and highly respected hosts which I did not want to happen. I think this effect could be caused by differences in ethical standards, attitudes, cultural backgrounds and life experiences. However, I would like to share in brief my impressions with my colleagues who came through a similar experience studying in the USA.

It's not a new idea that life of any society may be compared to a life a human being. It comes through the same stages of individual evolution—

babyhood, childhood, puberty, youth, adolescence, maturity, aging, death - and displays similar qualities at similar stages. Each of the stages implies development of some conventional traits of character, mastering of particular areas of existence. Everyone comes through these stages and everyone does it in his/her own specific way. Societies, cultures and civilizations live through these stages of ontogenesis as well. Some of them came through these stages more or less successfully and died, as the case is with Byzantium, Ancient Rome and Greece. Some are now experiencing the period of aging–as Britain, France, China and Japan. Some are just babies, as the former USSR. The latter, being born through Caesar section (a revolution) appeared to be not strong enough to live even to the period of childhood.

I had to resort to this "lyrical tour into American history" to explain in symbolic images my understanding of "American mind" as a social and historic phenomenon. For me it's a mind of a growing child, in all its possible manifestations, both positive and negative. And the central idea of it is that of development, i.e. self- and world- cognition, the process of learning. What qualities should a child develop to come over this stage successfully? What skills should one master to be able to win the struggle for knowledge? It is exactly the qualities, so typical of the American national character, and they are these:

1) Observativeness and inquisitiveness, analyticity – from here derives deep interest of the society to the issues of education and upbringing and a high overall educational level of its people;
2) Sociability and communicativeness which allow multiculturalism, pluralism and diversity;
3) Restlessness, creativeness and assertiveness, sometimes transforming into aggressiveness leading to confrontations with the world–hence conflicts in Vietnam, Korea, Persian Gulf, Yugoslavia and now Iraq.
4) Invincible optimism, high self-esteem and positive thinking – traditional American values highly respected in the world.

Still, the key-issue in the child's personal development is that of self-identification, achieving the awareness of one's own place in the world and understanding one's own values and life mission. That's why a little girl by the name of America is so preoccupied with the issues of race, gender and class – she needs to solve them to answer the eternal human questions – who she is and where she is going.

Wyoming Experiences of a Siberian Botanist

Yelena Kosovich

– Russia –

As one of JFDP's participants, from August, 2003 through July, 2004 I had the honor to work on this program. I was realizing my project within the frame of the JFDP academic field of environmental studies at the University of Wyoming (UW) Botany Department, Laramie. Working as a Docent of Irkutsk State University (ISU), Irkutsk, teaching botany courses at the Department of Botany and Genetics.

For the beginning, I have to tell that the trip to the Unites States in 2003 under the auspices of JFDP, American Councils For International Education/ ACTR&ACCELS, was not "my first discovery" of America. It was my third trip to the U.S.A. which is why my "cultural shock" that everyone inevitably experiences upon arrival in the U.S. for the first time was limited "only" by 3 points. First. Such a long – 11 months! – stay in America! The thought that my third experience to be expected as my longest trip to "another planet" strongly overloaded me, especially in the beginning. Second. Completely new impressions from the state of Wyoming – features of its culture, traditions, people, nature, etc. By that time, I, though, could be proud with my "personal" acquaintance with no less than half of American states, namely in Wyoming, I have never been before. Peasant, country-side remote corner of civilization, the right place to exile – I am sorry to say so, but this is how I perceived Wyoming during the very first days of my stay there. Desert all around (that shocked me as a botanist), unbelievable drought of the climate, the very bright (just like lamp in surgery room!) sun, severe wind plus high altitude (8 000 and more feet above sea level), clouds kind of laying on our shoulders, almost full absence of population (except us, poor trainees and … squirrels)… These are my and other Russian JFDPers first impressions of Wyoming. I have to note, these unexpected "beauties" of the Wild West evoked in us, newly arrived Russians, not the worst form of cultural shock – much humor and healthy laughter. This condition would periodically visit me all during my Wyoming experience. But, I have to add, finally, at the end of this experience, myself, along with my Russian friends, would just fall in love with this strange country with its unique nature, people, original history and traditions (Wyoming Randevouz as several day tour across the whole state, organized by the UW President for newly arrived trainees, would be very informative in this sense!). ...To say more, much later, this state would become the essential part of my personal life.

And last but not the least kind of my "cultural shock"–for the first time, I had to get involved into American university life, where I had to become a temporary part of UW Botany Department staff for a pretty long while (9 months of academic program plus, as the future showed, 2 months of my internship here). I acquired an awful lot of obligations including future presentations about my home country, Irkutsk University and Baikal (several months later, I would be proud to report to my Irkutsk colleagues on the phone about three quite good presentations). According to my academic plan, I had to explore traditions of the UW including student life and University communities. Attending teaching methodology courses at UW Ellbogen Center for Teaching and Learning let alone botany and ecologo-botanical classes would become my regular practice, etc. I have to mention, upon our arrival to Laramie, adapting to the beginning of our new life got UW International Program Office and, in particular, our Project Coordinator and just nice and exclusively helpful person Shawn Bunning. Thanks to him our problem with dwelling was solved very quickly. He acquainted us with UW structure, the plan of involving us in community life, making our transition to new life much smoother. Shawn and other people from the UW International Program Office all during our stay at the UW would be exclusively helpful to us, Russian JFDPers. At the UW Botany Department I also would meet hospitable people, both professors and students who would help me with setting uo my working space, kind advice, equipment for my research and readiness to have me as a trainee at their classes.

Since the very beginning of school year (when involved in the university and department life, attending classes, communicating with botany colleagues, attending monthly Friday scientific seminar, exploring vegetation of Laramie surroundings by myself and while at field classes (such as class of Vegetation Ecology by Dr. E. Pendal), step by step, I started getting the feeling that my placement was more than satisfactory and it is, undoubtedly, the merit of the JFDP recruitment policy of taking into account professional ambitions/ features of the future JFDPer. One of the reasons to think like that was the fact that I was embraced into the highly qualified community of my botany colleagues. All during the school year I had the chance to observe the process of teaching botanical courses and the use of modern teaching methodology by professors of one of the most professional Botany Departments in the Western United States which is the UW Botany Department. I got the chance to use the rich resources of the UW such as modern equipment, an excellent library, electronic and interlibrary resources. I was provided with all necessary to develop my curriculum on classical and modern botanical courses advancing my teaching strategy in Plant Systematic, Plant Anatomy, Summer Field Practical Course, etc. Of new teaching methods I was especially impressed with, I would mention PowerPoint presentation and student-led discussions.

Plant Anatomy course tought at UW by a geneticist (Dr. A.Sylvester) for juniors and provided with modern equipment for students' research, also involving Botany conservatory/garden of live plants facilities benefited my classes of Plant Anatomy by revealing the deeper approaches to the material. As for Professors S.Miller's and S.Jackson's class "Plant and Civilization", it was just great - full of extremely useful information on ways that plants have influenced the development of human civilization. Some creative ideas made this class very memorable for me: can you imagine the crowd of students in a lecture situation, chewing different kinds of bread offered by a teacher, in attempt to estimate its quality and identify its ingredients?!

The course of Botanical Nomenclature tought at UW by the leading plant taxonomists of Western U.S., Professors G.K.Brown and R.L.Hartman, based on the modern and classical foreign publications (that are mostly unavailable for us in my home university) and updated International Code of Botanical Nomenclature, also evoked my vivid interest. I was very curious to listen to professor-student discussions on Stearn's "Botanical Latin", which is a kind of "bible" for American plant taxonomists and one of the principal textbooks for American botany students. And, of course, since my first communication with American botanists (it happened many moons ago, as I was a participant of the American Association for the Advancement of Science expedition on Baikal) challenged me by the "American grammatical style" of reading of botanical Latin names, namely in Dr.R. Hartman's class I was trying to find out the "truth" in terms of this problem. I have to acknowledge, Dr.Hartman and I finally did not come to a mutually satisfactory point regarding the rules of reading scientific Latin plant names. Unfortunately, under such cases it is pretty difficult to rely on Latin as the international language of scientific communication. Judge for yourself, that scarcely, when hearing the word "Naiesee" said by an American bryologist, his/her European colleagues would be able to understand that it just implies the ordinary Mniaceae family.

Anyway, in my opinion, there should be some universal rules in scientific Latin to follow.

Modern methodology of ecobotanical field research of the courses of Vegetation Ecology (Dr. E.Pendall) and Field Ecology (by Dr. Meyer) as well as my internship experience with my colleagues from the Wyoming Natural Diversity Database (WyNDD) were very useful in developing the sections of natural ecosystem protection, the effect of management decision, and plant conservation of my summer field botany course on Lake Baikal. The manual "Educational Field Practical Course on Botany at the Bolshie Koty Biostation", written partly on the basis of my JFDP experiences, has been published by the Irkutsk University Publishing House in 2005.

To a botanist and ecologist as I am, Wyoming, with its rich biodiversity and world renowned national parks, is a great place to explore. Thanks to UW International Program Office staff and, in particular, Shawn Bunning, who organized these trips for us, international students, I had the exclusive chance to visit the protected areas of Rocky Mountain, Grand Teton and Yellowstone National parks and observe vegetation condition there and learn the methods of the whole ecosystem and plant species protection. I felt my readiness to be involved in environmental projects in WY and, in a little while, my wish came true.

Soon after my arrival there, I found out, as a bryologist, I can be useful to my WY botany colleagues since bryophytes is one of the least explored group of plants here. The idea of bryophyte inventory of one of the protected areas of WY, namely Medicine Bow-Routt National Forest (MB-RNF) later became the topic of my internship. I have to note, this experience advanced me professionally in the meaningful degree. My 2 month long internship became one of the most essential parts of my experience as a JFDPer. My research was done within the frame of the project of WyNDD on fens within the territory of MB-RNF. I was involved in the project as a bryology expert. Also, it was of my professional interest to learn methods of field research of fen sites used by my American colleagues. Of new modern methods, I'd like to specifically mention the usage the GPS in the field work, which is very helpful to exactly determine plant/plant community localities geographic parameters. (Since then, I do not understand how come many of my Russian botany colleagues still keep working without this irreplaceable for botanical research device!). Of my American colleagues, who were especially helpful in the field, I'd like to mention the true enthusiast of WY botany Bonnie Heidel, WyNND, the President of Wyoming Native Plant Society, I was really lucky to work with. Under her guidance, we took several unforgettable trips, very informative and full of bright impressions, each time discovering the beauty of WY nature, sometimes, though, dangerous: at times, while we were trying to get to the particular fen, our paths crossed with those of wild mountain lion and bears and we were close to meet them... in other cases, severe snow storm (such a characteristic for June in Wyoming!) stopped our jeep on the narrow serpentine-like steep road of the Snowy Range! Even now, two years later, I am recalling this unique experience with the same trepidation! The total number of bryophyte specimens collected by me all during those tours was as many as 900, no less. As Bonnie was joking, I had collected mosses by kilograms, rather than by envelopes/packets as it has to be. It is worthy to say, that shortly before I started my internship, I was provided with the legal permission to collect plants within the territory of the protected area of MBN-BF. As for the consequent material/collections processing, it was done under Professor William A. Weber (The University of Colorado, Boulder) supervising, who is a well-known plant systematicist and expert on bryophytes of the Rocky Mountain area. As result of my research, there have been some contributions to the WY bryology, namely, findings of some rare to the state of Wyoming and new to Albany County moss species. My collections made addition to the following herbaria of the USA and Russia: UW Rocky Mountain Herbarium, MB-RNF Herbarium, The University of Colorado Herbarium, Irkutsk State University Herbarium. My lists of fen bryoflora of Medicine Bow-Routt National Forest with the proper comments are being cited in the report of my American colleagues (Heidel, B. and G. Jones, in process [2006]. Botanical and ecological characteristics of fens on the Medicine Bow Mountains, Medicine Bow National Forest, Albany and Carbon counties, Wyoming. Prepared for the Medicine Bow-Routt National Forest. Wyoming Natural Diversity Database, University of Wyoming, Laramie, WY).

At the end of my note, summarizing my experience as a JFDPer, I would like to tell the following. Once again, I would like to extend my gratitude to the JFDP staff and, in particular, international offices of our institutions for their constant help and care of us, JFDPers, during our experiences in the USA, understanding and support of each of us and personal approach. Special appreciation goes to all institutions and individuals who organized for us very informative conferences in Minnesota and Washington DC., for giving us the chance to get invaluable experience of not only professional, but also interpersonal communication with Americans, also with representatives of the other nations and Russian colleagues involved in the JFDP program. With great respect, we appreciate the importance of the activities of American

Councils of International Education. By administering such international programs as JFDP this organization serves the global aim of dispersing intercultural and educational experience throughout the world and, hence, the noble mission of better mutual understanding of people in our multipolar world.

My American Experience

Saltanat Kazhimuratova

– Kazakhstan –

Americans eat only hamburgers and cheeseburgers. This was my impression on my first visit to the US about ten years ago. Another thing I noticed at that time was connected with a hotel. Whenever I stayed at the hotel, they changed my soap bars and shampoo and towels every day. Even if I had some shampoo left in the bottle, next day I always found a new soap bar and a new shampoo. I wondered why they didn't economize; I could have used these things one more time. And I concluded that America might be a very rich and developed country and they don't bother much about such small things as soaps and a bottle of shampoo in the hotels. They think about something big like politics and oil. I didn't hear them talking much about education. Neither had they bothered learning about your country. When I introduced myself and named my country, they had a vague idea about its location. Sometimes they mixed it up with Pakistan or Afghanistan or even Madagascar. I'm sorry to name all these facts but it really happened when I was here 10 years ago.

What has changed? What are my impressions now? What is my experience after five months there? Let me tell you what I personally did to improve things and use my stay in the U.S. to benefit both the American people and myself. First of all, some words about changes. Now I know that Americans eat other food too. They eat porridges, soups and salads. I was surprised to find ingredients for our traditional food. Almost in every big store you can see an aisle "International Food" and find at least something that reminds you of your own food.

During my stay in the hotel this time, I found a note asking to use the towel one more time if you think you could do it. In the next paragraph they explained the reason of such a request: hundreds of barrels of water used for washing towels and human resources, etc. Yes, economy! Hey, look, they are concerned about economy!

Once I was watching TV and saw an advertisement "No Child Left Behind". I told to myself: Yes, now they are thinking about education. Later I've observed a lot of discussions in newspapers and on TV revealing the great concern of the American people about the future of education. Another time I was surprised by the government's call for studying foreign languages and learning more about other cultures. It motivated me to become a contributor to this challenge.

I traveled by Greyhound bus and had lots of experiences and discovered a different America. In the bus stations I heard English, Spanish, Chinese and other languages. I have met people with various purposes of travel. Some were going to relatives in another state, others were looking for a job (like a young couple from Cuba, who could not find a job in Grand Rapids and were going to Miami in hopes of something better). These Americans could not afford to travel by their own cars (as they don't have any) or by plane (that is very expensive for them) and had no choice but to travel by inexpensive bus. I saw how tired they were as their trips sometimes lasted two or three days. Most of them had many kids and large baggage. This was also a kind of experience for me to see a traveling America.

Being a cultural agent, I introduced my country and its traditions to many people here. I have used every chance to talk about Kazakhstan and its development. When I met people, the first question I asked was "Have you heard about Kazakhstan?" or "What did you hear about my country?" Sometimes I was surprised as more people heard and knew. Moreover, they could give examples, like "Baikonur cosmodrome" or "your flag is blue with yellow sun" or, this info was very new and exciting for me, "it's mentioned in the last episode of "The West Wing TV show". Wow! Somebody here is helping me to introduce my country. I researched about this show and really found out that Kazakhstan is involved in some episodes of the West Wing show's last season.

Also I offered a list of useful phrases in Kazakh and taught them my language. Later on some students and professors greeted me in Kazakh. I was so happy when I heard them saying "Salamatsyz ba!"(Good afternoon! (formal) or "Sau bolynyz! (Good bye!). It really sounded warm and welcoming.

The most significant professional achievement was my participation and presentation in the United Nations conference on Central Asia in the Utah Valley State College. This conference gathered a distinguished group of high-ranking people – ambassadors, U.S. State Department officials, experts, scholars, and diplomats. I was the only representative from Kazakhstan. At the conference I have really become an Ambassador of my country and felt a great responsibility. This was a very exciting and demanding task I have ever had before.

While being in Utah, I have explored a new state and discovered new things about the United States. I lived in a large (not typical for America) family – there were three daughters and one son. But my colleague's host family was bigger – ten children. I observed the respect and value of the family. This was a very remarkable similarity to my people's values. Another interesting fact: as soon as I arrived at Salt Lake City Airport and saw mountains around, I asked myself: where am I? Am I in my city Almaty? The nature of Utah, particularly, mountains resembled so much my Kazakhstan. I was surprised to find this similarity.

My host family was eager to learn about our part of the world and we talked till late nights. I cooked traditional food and shared recipes. We sang songs in English and Russian, played Kazakh and American music. I taught them Kazakh language. This was a wonderful experience!

In the School of Journalism at Michigan State University I enjoyed the classes and people around. On March 22 we celebrated together Nauryz, the Kazakh New Year. I invited my American colleagues to a Kazakh "dastarkhan" (a bountiful holiday table) and demonstrated some food and symbols of the country. My colleagues liked the idea of having such an event and decided to make it traditional in the school to learn about other cultures. Thus, I become a pioneer in promoting the cultural understanding between different ethnics.

I am sure that benefited much from the JFDP program and my stay in the U.S. Both professional and personal undertakings were huge and fruitful and rewarding. I would miss the university campus with squirrels; students wearing t-shirts and short pants, and sandals without socks and not caring about the windy and cold weather; Americans always drinking everything with ice (brr!); will miss hearing "yep!"; and will remember the life of a "visiting international scholar" that was full of events and impressions

I am very happy that had this opportunity to come and see the United States again after ten years later – the country of contrast and diversity, the country of similarities and differences and the country of hopes and achievements.

Labor Day

Sergei V. Arkhipov, PhD

– Russia –

International cooperation has already impacted on many Russian university educators. The example is my own professional development. During career I went through all the basic stages of practical and teaching work in Mass Communications. At the early stages of my employment I worked as a senior correspondent at the respected Russian regional daily, conducted my personal broadcastings through local TV. Tens documentaries have been shot according to my screen versions by North-Caucasus Studio of Documentaries. Later on I started working as Assistant Professor and delivered seminar studies on Journalism, Literary, and the Art at North-Ossetian State University (NOSU).

Afterward I became Senior Lecturer and read courses on vide range of disciplines in Mass Media and Literature, published outcome of my research, and supervised students' summer internship. Now I work as an Associate Professor at the department of Russian Literature at NOSU and conduct courses on Literature and Journalism as well as redact interuniversity collection of articles in social science and humanities.

I considerably widened my pedagogical and research skills by means of experience at the University of Tennessee, Knoxville, in 1998-1999. Such practice for an academic year gave me new links with educators in the United States, Ukraine, and Kazakhstan. Having become a finalist of Junior Faculty Development Program (JFDP) financed by American government through the United States Information Agency (now Bureau of Educational and Cultural Affairs of the United States Department of State) and directly ran by means of orders through American Councils for International Education (ACTR/ACCELS) I have got unique scholastic and pedagogical experience that is a combination of Russian and American teaching and research methods. Two months internship at the largest Russian literary quarterly abroad–New York City quarterly "The New Review" widened my circle of acquaintances with those well-known Russian and American scholars, writers, poets, and journalists living in or close to New York City. My speeches at a number of scholastic conferences as well as lectures and publications about media and literature in the USA were the outcome of such internship.

After coming home from the United States I without stopping my extensive pedagogical practice at NOSU could organize department of Mass Communications at non-governmental Vladikavkaz Institute of Economics, Management, and Law (NGO VIEML) and get governmental licenses to teach Public Relations (PR) and Advertising. My new skills allowed me set up about a dozen of new workplaces for highly qualified professors. In 2006 my team consisted of many alumni of the US sponsored exchange programs got accreditation PR specialty and put on the job marketplace the first graduates with PR diploma in hands.

During my classes I usually say to students that they could get their marketable qualification in PR due to the help of the personnel of ACTR/ACCELS as well as many American professors and scholars. I often speak to them about the people, places, and towns that I met during my visit to the United States.

Time pointers on my hand watch showed 6 PM when we drove up into the suburb of Knoxville, TN. Day heat slowly began to step back and the holiday crowd of townspeople has already gathered here to celebrate Labor Day. It was very conveniently to all of them looking at the salute from the height section of the bridge across sufficiently wide river.

The southerners each year come here from the different towns and villages of Tennessee on the first Monday of September to admire dozen of minutes with colorful spectacle - the game of a man with the fire against the dark background of the sky. It was necessary to wait several hours when the complete darkness falls down, but there was not already vacant place in the area. Fords, Buicks, and Toyotas blocked everything with importantly looking travelers having a sit near them before their expandable tables.

We have taken provision away from a trunk and left the part of our companions to delight with the coolness in shadow of trees and went downward to the road for a walk. There was something like we usually say in Russian slang *tusovka*–that means the gathering of people coming in for an entertainment. The well-dressed citizens in the expectation of the first volley slowly walked along the freeway blocked for all vehicles for a period of salute.

At one stroke I saw many summer commercial tents located along the entire road curb. Judging by the ads placed on them, I supposed that they all traded snacks, drinks, and some other food.

However instead of trade young people inside simply gave out packs of chips for free to everybody. They gave out as a rule two bright small packets to anybody who has approached to their tents.

> There were five-six persons in average in a queue near these tents. The queue rapidly moved and some citizens, having received two small packets, went into its tail again and took back new portion of salt dainty in a couple of minutes.

In a little while I wanted to drink. And I quickly realized it that beverages were sold in the other distantly standing tents, but at the almost predatory price at that time - two dollars for one plastic bottle of Coca-Cola. Far much noticeable queue has appeared near these tents. Cash dollars rapidly moved away from the wallets of gathered here townspeople into the cashboxes of enterprising young guys.

Soon people quickly understood their commercial craftiness. After giving salt chips to public for free the trading guys four times more expensively sold beverages to public. But to purchase the cold soda on the regular price in this distant area was not possible.

No one of the visitors got anger. They all voluntarily took free chips and some of them have taken so many small packets that they were not accommodated in the fingers spread widely and, after having eat them all, four times more expensively they paid for each bottle of cold soda.

- The sharks of capitalism business, - in such terms I sadly estimated the guys' marketing strategy counting available cash in my wallet.

I almost forgot about this case in a month. Early Saturday morning I came up to the downtown park in Knoxville. There have already been assembled about two dozen of volunteers. Some days before we agreed to take part in charitable market during weekend and to send money earned from the sale of souvenirs, beverages, beer, and snacks to organize Tennessee Special Olympics for disabled children.

Earlier I never worked in the trade, however as soon as I have known the final goal of that market, I sufficiently joyfully observed my developing skills to open bottles in large quantity with Bud, Coca, and Pepsi. In the meantime my verbose assistant from Ukraine prepared hotdogs for customers. She put sausage in the sliced roll and poured it heavily with spicy sauce.

At the same time she shared with me her information about advanced beauty shops in the suburb, dates of opening the biggest sales, addresses of popular matchmaker sites, and so on. In all this stuff she knew sense; however she has not been experienced better than I in the retail trade. From time to time she accidentally let fall a roll to the earthen floor, then-a sausage, and afterward-everything together. When she gets down to raise a sandwich I carelessly dripped her with the water. She hypocritically shouted, but did not stop dropping something to the earth from time to time.

Some portion of her lightness has transferred to me and from time to time we moved away from the tent to have a dance in the entire confidence that we have already done a good deal assembling sufficient amount of money to send several disabled children to the Special Olympics. Moreover we both have a ground for pride. Some less hardly motivated fellows arrived with us in the morning to work in the park did not carry out the stress of physical labor and they already returned their food to other participants of this philanthropic action and left us long hours ago.

Staying at the work site longer than some others, I unexpectedly felt that a familiar sense has begun returning to me. Last time I experienced it in the Caucasus Mountains in Russia. After graduation from the university I invited two my college mates to live several weeks in the alpine camp. To reach it I made a long journey together with them by the train right through the whole country. When we arrived into the camp there had already been about thirty of mountain climbers and usual tourists from many Russian regions. Once an instructor proposed to all of us to make the two days trip into the mountains. The bored with longer stay in the hotel people quickly get off for a way.

The road was truly difficult one. The narrow path overgrown on the edges with fern steeply pulled upward. Pushing my body through it I caught with fingers for the cliff in order my heavy knapsack with the food, warm cloth, and tent would not drop me down into the deep precipice. Fast mountain river in the gorge being rolled across the fixed boulders threatened our group with loud roar from underneath. Its monotonic noise slightly muffled complaints of my university mates on the difficulty of the way and heaviness of their burden. It seemed to me that they were completely exhausted by the end of the first day of our journey. During the night halt the instructor proposed them both to have a rest in the camp next day. The fellows denied all my persuasions to continue way upward and stayed on the clearing in the tent camp.

Early next morning I along with several other fellows began to clamber again into the mountain. As soon as we have reached the apex I breathed fresh air into my breast. Nothing something special: deep breath–and expiration. But the sense of confidence overfilled me. After standing on the vertical cliff several minutes I moved downward with my new acquaintances. On the way back I have met my companions waited for us. In the contrast with my new acquaintances their faces expressed a set of negative emotions-malice, offence, bitterness, fatigue, and disappointment...

Scarcely talking, we rapidly gathered the remaining things into the knapsacks, rolled up the tents, and left temporary camp. Back way to the hotel seemed to me twice as easily and shorter. Nothing strange. I have been to the mountain peak.

The same cool sense of confidence I felt again as soon as I realized that many volunteers had already left us long hours ago to have a rest. Time approached 10 PM while I with my energetic and talkative assistant continued to work. In spite of her lightness for an effect the girl proved to be persistent person and she obviously did not want to leave working place earlier me.

However there were increasingly less buyers in the park. The trade went limply by the end of the light day. But it goes pretty good only near adjacent tent. The guys, who worked into it, could compete with a vending machine in the speed of servicing the customers. During the whole day small pick-ups regularly drove up to them and supplied them with beverages, snacks, chocolate, cakes, and other provisions. Their products would be sufficient amount to me for several days of active trade. But they placed new order every several hours–and new pick-up drove up to their tent again, which the guys rapidly unloaded. Sometimes, I spoke to them while there was not anybody around. But as soon as new buyer approached our leisurely conversation attenuated.

Finally, such late time came up as all visitors disappeared in the urban park. Under the light of automobile headlights we began to displace tents and load commercial equipment and remaining provision into the pick-ups. Next day early in the Sunday morning everybody have to come here again and spend another day selling cold soda, beer, sandwiches, chips, and all possible food in order to earn more funds to lease a stadium, purchase supply materials, sport clothing, and souvenirs. Later on they have to reward all these prizes under the flashes of many cameras to handicapped children emotively being glad because of their success at the Special Olympics. For me the day of charitable labor was finished that night. Next morning I was going to take a trip by air to another state for a conference.

I started counting the gain of 137 dollars. It was not much for the entire day of trade. However, it was already too late to increase the sum, so I went off to return money to the organizers of a charitable festival. There already stood up several guys near them. Talking over between each over, they entrusted their daily income–just about 300 dollars. It was twice as much as I did!

The more successful fellows were my neighbors. The entire day they worked very hard: All the daylong they slicing rolls, filling plastic glasses, unlocking bottles, and so on. They never moved away for a dance, for a break, or just to stretch the legs. After carefully looking at their faces I resolved that I have already seen these guys somewhere else.

I was trying to remember them. As much as I was looking on them I grow in confidence that they were the same boys, who a month ago on the Labor Day gave out chips for free and sold each plastic bottle of cold Coca-Cola for two dollars later.

Strangely enough, but the sharks of capitalism were working along with many other citizens as simple volunteers the whole day! It was very untypical for Russia. Our new sharks of capitalism business as well as majority of officials in past Soviet times usually preferred to watch on the physically consuming labor of volunteers only through the glasses of their luxury vehicles or modern offices. They habitually tried to organize unpaid work for the profit of the whole country the day before such national holidays as The First of May, The Victory Day on 9th May, on new holiday on the 12th of June, and on some other days. But I have never seen them or ordinary citizens working until deep night for the advantage of homeless and disabled children or somebody else.

Usually organizational personnel in my home country come up for such kind of voluntary work as collecting a garbage in a park or painting in white color trunks of trees in a street for a couple of hours only after listening multiple treats of being fired or some other repressive measures from the administration. People in Russia even coined special oxymoron for such kind of labor–*dobrovol'no-prinuditel'niy trud,* which could be interpreted as forced-voluntary work. Meanwhile coerced working for free people usually quickly left for good their temporary job places just after midday check-up organized by their supervisors.

In Knoxville I have seen for the first time in my life absolutely another attitude of citizens toward voluntary work. Nobody compelled somebody to stay at the working site extra hours. Citizens contributed as much time for the Special Olympics as they have available and all volunteers left their places just in time they wanted.

Why Americans work so hard, so long, and so free?

In order to realize it and to approve my suggestion about my neighbors I considered necessary to get close acquaintance with the fellows. I did approach to the guys and said that I arrived from Russia and could teach them one old good Russian saying.

- What kind of saying? - One of them asked me.
- *Greby otsuda,* - I answered in Russian.
- What does it mean?
- It is appropriate to say anybody *greby otsuda* when someone gives you back the small packet of chips and requires to sell him a bottle of cold soda at a regular price, - I have said.

They all have a fun. Probably my suggestion was true and they were at the bridge on the last Labor Day. We have recalled excellent spectacle. I did not see earlier such beautiful ornaments of fire in the night sky. I did not also see before that the people fleeced credulous citizens through several weeks later were working free of charge for their benefit with the same huge energy.

Finally I got an answer only the first part of my question. Having a talk with those guys, I almost certainly comprehended something important in the character of the Americans. For example, here these guys! They can hardly ever articulate major differences in the political programs of Republicans and Democrats, sometimes they may pucker forehead before showing Russia on the global map, but when the matter concerns their persuasions, somewhat they piously believe in these guys turn out to be inflexible and obstinate.

Throughout their life they will work hard for the benefit not only their own families but also for the men and women with whom they grow up in American county side. And as soon as an issue concerns physically consuming travel by walk they will take upon themselves the heaviest load. And if they will some day go together to the mountains I have no doubts they all reach the peak and nobody stay in the camp to have a rest. And I do not know is there anything in the world that could change their attitude…

Unfortunately, I did not get answer the second part of my question and grasped it whether those twisted credulous citizens round little finger on Labor Day a month later worked as volunteers for Special Olympics or there was just another group?

In any case it does not concern me at all, because I got much important knowledge.
…We departed from the park deeply in the night. Organizers of the Special Olympics presented me special T-shirt with many emblems of the festival. In Russia it reminds me about that event. Names of many firms and organizations are drawn on it along with brands of all the sponsors of Special Olympics. There are such large enterprises as Wal-Mart, national banks, TV channels, insurance companies and such small organizations as local credit unions, bakeries, groceries, restaurants, high and middle schools.

I looked like a racer of "Formula-1" in it because of many advertisements painted on the t-shirt. But I hardly ever put it on. The t-shirt had a very large size for me. It seemingly tells me that I took upon myself too difficult responsibility at that time.   Actually, I did not often participate in charitable actions in my hometown. In Russia professors could stand in a queue for a cup of free soup because of low salary. But I usually work hard at two different jobs. Besides I teach additional courses beyond university. No longer have I walked into the mountains. But sometimes I travel.

During one trip I met in a hotel a young woman on the similar T-shirt fitted to her pretty good. She was a dancer from the southern Russian town. On the first glance she was a live clone of the famous Barbie doll. She has bright red hair, polished nails, and bloom on her cheeks a-la Santa Claus. I introduced myself and asked whether she really did something for the Special Olympics?

- My former boy friend gave this T-shirt when I was living in Texas, - she answered. – He often participated in charitable actions. He was my partner for the classical dances for several years. He purchased me many ball dresses. When we moved apart I returned him all the dresses. But I occasionally saved this T-shirt.
- What do you do in Russia? - I inquired.
- I taught English at the university for several years. But now I usually engaged in private coaching schoolboys to make out their foreign language assignments for a class. I also do translations to and from English.
- It is strangely enough. You could achieve much more in Russia with Texas diploma.
- At first my career was rather successful one. The students loved me. But the dances were guilty in my failure.
- Does it really so?
- Yes, that is right! I have noticed that people in our town rarely associated with each other. To improve this I planned to organize a dance club. I wanted to make dances the form of social interactions. At first we gathered and danced only with the students. Then their parents and friends jointed us. Several times I moved to the summer school in Scotland. I have studied Scottish dances over there. I have been even accepted as a member into the Royal Society of Scottish dancers. I always moved there only during my leave in the summer. But somebody at the university did not like my frequent dance tours abroad. They began to pursue me. Soon I was fired... I do live difficultly now without a constant work, but I do perceive myself as a free person.
- Do you regret about that?
- You know, everything seems go wrong to me when I walk to the dance club in the night. I think that I did not succeed in the life. I did not want even to glance at somebody. But I quickly realize it that many people were waiting for me in the club. They were simply standing near the hall wall and waiting, because many of them were very lonely and had no place to go for any entertainment at all in the night. I usually do approach to them, greet them, and I start next lesson.
- So, you just give the lessons of Scottish dances to citizens...
- These are not regular lessons. Lonely people come to the club not only for a dance, but also to socialize with each other. And I work as a bridge between them. I usually run around the city and search for the hall to rent it and then I prepare a leasing contract. In a month its owner throw us into the street, because we usually could not pay high lease fee by the deadline. And, I started again going around the whole city to find another dance hall for our group. Sometimes we organize public performance, but always free of charge. You know, I would like to make dances the form of socializing our citizens. People should not pay for it.

That day I had a long conversation. She was the alumnus of recognizable graduate fellowship program. So we have a lot to talk about. We have exchanged of opinions about visiting Tennessee, Texas, Chicago, and New York. The "doll" turned out to be very interesting person with apparently not easy destiny. After that conversation I have not met this fiery-red hair dancer somewhere again. At home I named in her honor one of my files in the folder "My Documents". Sometimes opening it I recall Tennessee, Special Olympics, Labor Day, salute in Knoxville, different conferences, meetings, speeches.

And at that time I comprehend that my travel to America was full of sense, because many people around got new perspective, confidence, and qualification brought to Russia by every alumnus after coming home from the United States.

The Contributors

Larisa Chuprina – Ukraine

Lchuprin@hotmail.com

Larissa Chuprina was a JFDP scholar during 1996-1997. She is interested in different aspects of education for adults including ESL/EFL, cross-cultural communication & adjustments, comparative adult education, and international education. She is being involved in Train-the-Trainer Program in Ukraine and the USA. Larissa is currently a Visiting Professor in one of the American Universities.

Pavel V. Sysoyev – Russia

psysoyev@yahoo.com

Pavel V. Sysoyev is a professor of American Studies & Applied Linguistics and a Founding Director of the Foreign Language Poly-cultural Education Research Laboratory at Tambov State University, Russia. He holds a Master of Arts in TESOL from the Pennsylvania State University (1999), Ph.D. in Applied Linguistics from Tambov State University (1999), and Ed.D in Foreign Language Pedagogy from Moscow State University named after M. Lomonosov (2004). He is a recipient of *President Boris Yeltsin's Research Scholar Award* (1998), and *the Most Active Scholar of the Russian Federation* (Soros Foundation, 2003). Dr. Sysoyev has written extensively on the cultural dimensions of foreign language teaching. Among his recently published books are: *Theory of Foreign Language Poly-cultural Education*, winner of the Silver Medal of the All-Russian Exhibition Center VDNH (Moscow, Euro-school Press, 2003), *Identity, Culture, and Language Teaching* (University of Iowa, 2002), and -*Multicultural America: Teaching about Cultural Diversity in the United States* (Moscow, Euro-school Press, 2005). More recently, Euro-school Press published his textbook for upper secondary schools *US Culture and Society* (2005), which was recommended by the Russian Ministry of Education to be used as an American Studies textbook on the secondary level. Dr. Sysoyev's non-academic life revolves around his family and friends.

Azim Bayzoev - Tajikistan

bayzoev@gmail.com

Dr. Azim Bayzoev is a JFDP Fellow (The University of Kansas, Women Studies Program) from Tajikistan. He has a PhD on Oriental Studies (Tajik State University, Dushanbe, Tajikistan) and Master on Law (Tajik Institute of Tax and Law). Azim Bayzoev currently teaches courses including *Persian Language, Theory and Practice in Translation* and *Gender Problems in Language and Literature* at the Oriental Department of the Tajik State National University. He is an author of 9 books including 5 textbooks and about 70 articles on Oriental Sciences, Linguistics, Educational Reforms and Gender Problems, published in Tajikistan, Russia, British Kingdom, the US, Pakistan, Iran, Kyrgyzstan and Afghanistan. Azim Bayzoev is also working as an education expert and the head-editor of an Educational Reforms Support Unit (NGO ERSU "PULSE") publication entitled "School and Society".

Alexey Konobeev - Russia

alexey_konobeiev@yahoo.com

Alexey Konobeev graduated with distinction from Tambov State University named after G.R. Derzhavin in 1998 with an undergraduate degree in Linguistics. While at the university, he took an English language course at the University of Northumbria, Newcastle-upon-Tyne, UK. After graduate studies course he received his PhD (Kandidat Nauk) degree from the same university in Applied Linguistics (English Language Teaching methodology). His main interests are teaching writing and research in writing (fiction, non-fiction, & academic writing). He has supervised two PhD theses and is actively working towards developing a discourse approach to teaching writing in Russia. He was a JFPD Fellow in 2004-2005 at Iowa State University, where he studied Creative Writing, Second Language Acquisition, Discourse Analysis and English for Specific purposes among other subjects. In 2004-2006 he worked as an Associate Director of the Institute for Supplementary

Education at Tambov State, as such supervising all international students in the university. Since September 2006 Alexey Konobeev has moved to the city of Obninsk to work as the vice editor-in-chief for TITUL Publishers, which publishes popular series of English language textbooks.

Aida Huseynova – Azerbaijan

anhuseynova@yahoo.com

Aida Huseynova is an Associate Professor of Musicology at the Baku Music Academy, Azerbaijan. She has graduated from Baku Music Academy in 1987, received her Ph.D. from Saint-Petersburg Conservatory, Russia in 1992. Since 2000, she has been visiting Indiana University, Bloomington to work on educational projects related to Azerbaijani music and culture. She was a JFDP scholar In 2001-2002 at Indiana University, Bloomington. She delivered numerous presentations in Indiana University, University of Chicago, Columbia University, Purdue University, University of Madison, Wisconsin, and Ohio State University in the U.S, and Cambridge University in U.K. She has also served as the member of the Advisors' Committee at the Sixth Annual San Francisco World Music Festival (San Francisco, 2005). She was musicologist-in-residence at the International Festival and Symposium of Contemporary music *Icebreaker III: The Caucasus* (Seattle, 2006) She is the Secretary General of the National Music Committee of Azerbaijan, and a member of the Composers Union of Azerbaijan and Central Eurasian Studies Society, U.S.A. She has authored more than 80 publications, including 4 books.

Natalia Kuznetsova – Russia

2natasha@mail.ru

Natalia Kuznetsova was a JFDP fellow in 2000-2001 at Pittsburgh State University with specialization in American Literature. Natalia received her PhD degree from St Petersburg Pedagogical University in 1995 and since then teaches English as a foreign language at Novgorod State University, Russia. She published two manuals on Text Analysis which are based on materials collected during her study in the USA and where she tried to combine both Russian and Western approaches to Text Analysis. At present she is writing her post-doctoral dissertation on V. Nabokov's American novels. In order to broaden her possibilities to work on her dissertation in the USA under some grant or scholarship, she has got the qualification for teaching Russian as a foreign language from Moscow State University in June, 2006.

Mirjana Bobic – Serbia

matildab@EUnet.yu

Dr. Mirjana Bobic is a JFDP alumna. In 2006 she spent the spring semester as a visiting faculty at Muskie School of Public Service, University of Southern Maine. She is an assistant professor at the Department of Sociology, Faculty of Philosophy Belgrade University, Serbia. She teaches social demography and population studies. Besides teaching, she is a researcher in the Institute for Sociological Research in Belgrade, Serbia. She also receives a lot of requests for consultancy work from Serbian Government, other official institutions and NGOs. Currently she is involved in pursuing an NGO project related to evolving health care system in Serbia.

Valentyna Arkhelyuk – Ukraine

arvalentina@mail.ru

Valentyna Arkhelyuk is an Associate Professor from Ukraine. She graduated from Chernivtsi National University (CNU) with a specialty in Romano-Germanic Languages & Literature. She is doing her research in the field of linguistics with a focus on Sociolinguistics & Cross-Cultural Communication. Valentyna was awarded the JFDP Scholarship in 2000. She has administrative experience working as an Associate Dean in the Foreign Languages Department in 2001-2003. As a University Academician and Department of Scientific & Methodical Council member she represented CNU at the International World of Education Exhibitions. She worked on the Accreditation Committee preparing scientific reports and material for national & international conferences. In addition, she serves as volunteer for leading seminars, organizing professional meetings, and participates in tutorial programs. Her other interests include traveling, sports, music, and art.

Oksana Maslovskaya – Russia

oksana_maslovskaya2002@yahoo.com

Oksana Maslovskaya is a JFDP alumna of 2002-2003. In 1991 she graduated from Far Eastern State Technical University, Vladivostok, Russia with honors. She was the teacher at her alma mater and practicing architect in private firm. After completion of her study and research at Landscape Architecture Program, Oklahoma State University, Stillwater, OK in 2002-

2003 Oksana Maslovskaya and her husband Grigoriy Ignatov established new Landscape Design Department in Vladivostok State University of Economy and Service. Now Oksana Maslovskaya is serving as an Associate Professor and trying to be a good mom for daughter Gallina, who was born in Oklahoma, and continuing to work on changing the natural and cultural landscape of her home city.

Yelena Kondaurova – Kazakhstan

klenart2004@yahoo.com

Yelena Kondaurova is a Junior Faculty Development Program scholar in 2004-05 from Kazakhstan. She joined School of Public and Environmental Affairs, Indiana University, Bloomington. Her projects besides attending classes at Arts Administration Program include arts management and music education. At home, Yelena is an Associate Professor at the Theory of Music Department, the Kazakh National Conservatory in Almaty. Since 1989 she teaches musical theoretical disciplines and Arts Management for Musicians there. She obtained her Ph.D (Art Criticism) degree from Fine Arts Academy Scientific Research Institute of Art Studies in Tashkent, Uzbekistan in 2002.

Maryna Babenko – Ukraine

maryna_babenko@hotmail.com

Maryna Babenko is a JFDP scholar from Ukraine. She possesses a PhD in Linguistics (Germanic Languages). Maryna graduated with distinction from the Department of Foreign Languages, Kharkiv National University, Ukraine. She has been a member of the English Philology Chair at the Kharkiv National Pedagogical University since 1994. Maryna has become a Deputy Dean of the Department of Foreign Philology at this University in 2002. Prior to that she has worked at the Foreign Languages Chair of Ukrainian Academy of Pharmacy. She has more than 20 years of experience in teaching English as a foreign language as well as in teachers' training. Her scientific interests are wide including semantics, history of English, and assessment in the language. In 1998 Maryna was awarded the annual TESOL/TEFL Travel Grant for the TESOL Convention, Seattle, WA, USA. She is the author of more than 35 scientific articles, methodical instructions, summaries, presentations at scientific and alumni conferences, and co-author of the textbook "English for Students in Pharmacy".

Rakhiya Bekbayeva – Kazakhstan

rakhiya@kimep.kz

Rakhiya Bekbayeva is a JFDP alumna of 2000. She received her undergraduate degree in Teaching English from Almaty Institute of Foreign Languages. She received graduate degree in International Journalism and Mass Communications from the Kazakhstan Institute of Management, Economics and Strategic Research (KIMEP) in Almaty. Currently, she works in KIMEP, teaching English to graduate students and Research Writing to undergraduates.

Alissa Tolstokorova – Ukraine

alicetol@yahoo.com

Alissa Tolstokorova is a JFDP alumna of 2000 from Kiev, Ukraine. She has a PhD in Humanities and Social Sciences. She currently holds a position of director of the centre for research on family and gender at the Public Institute for Family and Youth Issues of the Ministry of Ukraine for Family, Youth and Sports. Prior to this position she worked in gender policy consultancy and development in projects of the Ukrainian Institute for Social Research and Public Institute for Family and Youth Issues (Kiev, Ukraine). She has also provided services of a national consultant on gender policy and a planning expert to project on agricultural and rural policy development, carried out by the Ministry of Agrarian Policy of Ukraine. She held a position of an Associate Professor at the University of Economics and Law "KROK"(Kiev, Ukraine). She is a holder of international scholarships for research in Gender Studies at Stockholm University, Sweden (2004-2005), University of Leeds, UK (2003-2004), and George Mason University, USA (1999-2000). She is also authored more than 80 publications.

Yelena Kosovich – Russia

klenart2004@yahoo.com

Yelena Ivanovna Kosovich-Anderson is 2003-2004 JFDP alumna from Russia. She is working as a Docent/ Associate Professor of Irkutsk State University (ISU), Irkutsk, Siberia, at the Department of Botany and Genetics. She graduated from the same University in 1984. Most of her professional experience is teaching of general botany and bryology (a science on mosses and moss-like plants) at ISU and scientific exploration of bryophytes and vascular plants of protected areas of Baikal region. She is a bryophyte herbarium curator at ISU. Yelena is the author of over 70 papers, including 3 regional Red Data books of plants, scientific monographs, educational manuals and others on environmental and bryological topics. Yelena received her kandidatskaya degree in biology at Tomsk State University, Tomsk, one of the leading higher education institutions in Russia. In 1999, she worked at the field Museum of Botany in Chicago, IL, on a grant of the Field Museum Scholarship Program, Robert O. Bass Visiting Scientist Fund. In 2004, within the frame of her JFDP internship, she worked as an expert on bryophytes of Medicine Bow National Forest fens, WY.

Saltanat Kazhimuratova – Kazakhstan

saltanatedu@yahoo.com

Saltanat Kazhimuratova is a JFDP 2005-2006 Fellow from Kazakhstan. She is teaching in the Department of Journalism and Mass Communication at the Kazakhstan Institute of Management, Economics and Strategic Research (KIMEP), a western-style university in Almaty. Mrs. Kazhimuratova has eight years of professional experience as a journalist focused on social and political issues. Saltanat participated in the "Sustaining Democratic Press" editorial training program of the Thomson Foundation, UK. She has participated in a study tour of mass media in the USA, during which she visited ABC News, The Washington Post, Voice of America, Discovery Channel, NBC and others. Saltanat has two graduate degrees: one with honors from Pedagogical Institute and another in Journalism. She obtained her degree in Journalism at Kazakh State University after al-Farabi in Almaty. Mrs. Kazhimuratova is a member of Association for Education in Journalism and Mass Communication (AEJMC), Columbia, South Carolina, USA. She also joined the Central Eurasian Studies Society, Harvard Program on Central Asia and the Caucasus, Cambridge, MA, USA.

Sergei V. Arkhipov – Russia

sarkhipov@hotmail.com

Sergei Arkhipov is a Fulbright scholar. He works as an Associate Professor at the Department of Russian Literature at North-Ossetian State University and runs the Department of Mass Communications at NGO Vladikavkaz Institute of Economics, Management, and Law in Russia. Serhgei got his undergraduate diploma in Journalism from St.-Petersburg State University and defended thesis of Candidate of Science (that is Russian equivalent of American PhD) at Moscow State University. Now he teaches a wide range of courses including Introduction to Literary Studies, Pressing Problems in Modern Russian Literature and Journalism, Russian Satirical Literature at the End of 19th and Early of the 20th Centuries, Literary Journalism in Russia and USA, and Public Relations in Russia and the USA.

The Editors

Zeeshan-ul-hassan Usmani

zeeshan.usmani@yahoo.com

Zeeshan-ul-hassan Usmani is a Fulbright scholar. He has recently completed a master's in Computer Science at the Florida Institute of Technology. His area of interest includes swarm intelligence, self-organization and complex systems. Zeeshan has authored several articles and two books entitled *C/C++ with Object-Oriented Programming* and *USA: My Fulbright Experience published in 2001 and 2005.* He has also edited two books: *Experiencing America: Through the Eyes of Visiting Fulbright Scholars* and *Similarity in Diversity – Reflections of Malaysian and American Exchange Scholars.* He is also a member of IEEE (Institute of Electrical and Electronics Engineers), ACM (Association of Computing Machinery), and a chartered member of the BCS (British Computer Society). He lives in Princeton, NJ.

Tatyana Shadieva

tshadieva@wiut.uz

Tatyana Shadieva, originally from an ancient central Asian town of Bukhara, now lives and works in Tashkent, Uzbekistan. She was a Junior Faculty Development Program fellow at California State University, Long Beach in 2004-2005. Her interest includes, but not limited to, TEFL, inclusive and special education (visual impairment), literature and gender studies.

Imran Khanzada

Imran.khanzada@gmail.com

Imran Khanzada graduated from Wayne State University in Detroit. His areas of expertise are software consulting, business development and international marketing. He has worked in the software industry United Arab Emirates, Pakistan, United Kingdom, Canada and USA. He is interested in world politics and cultural diversity. He is also the member of IEEE, ACM, and INeta. He lives in Chicago, IL.

www.ingramcontent.com/pod-product-compliance
Lightning Source LLC
Chambersburg PA
CBHW061315280526
45784CB00002B/997